The Doctor and the Law

The Doctor and the Law

Second edition

J Leahy Taylor
MB, BS, DMJ, MRCGP
Secretary, The Medical Protection Society Limited, London

Pitman

PITMAN BOOKS LIMITED
128 Long Acre, London WC2E 9AN

PITMAN PUBLISHING INC.
1020 Plain Street, Marshfield, Massachusetts

Associated Companies
Pitman Publishing Pty Ltd, Melbourne
Pitman Publishing New Zealand Ltd, Wellington
Copp Clark Pitman, Toronto

First Published 1970
Second Edition 1982

British Library Cataloguing in Publication Data

Taylor, J. Leahy
The doctor and the law.—2nd ed.
1. Medical laws and legislation—Great Britain.
I. Title
344.104'41 KD3395

ISBN 0 272 79680 8

Text set in 10/12pt Linotron 202 Times, printed and bound in Great Britain at The Pitman Press, Bath

Contents

Foreword

Keith Simpson, MD, FRCP, FCPath,
Professor of Forensic Medicine in the University of London

'Dare quam accipere' was Thomas Guy's motto for the hospital he provided in London to give succour and skilled professional care for the ailing and the sick, and for thousands of doctors in all walks of practice this is a source of great content. Doctoring is a good life.

But professional practice is not all roses. The best intentions of doctors sometimes go awry. Mistakes mar the handling of patients, create errors in diagnosis, and spoil the chances of successful treatment. It is when these arise from a lack of care, failure to ensure accuracy in records or communications, or from a more serious disregard for ethical standards, that trouble is bound to follow. Patients who have sustained insult, endured unnecessary hurt or further ill-health, lost the wrong eye, tooth, or leg, and whose financial stability has suffered, have a right to litigation to recover some sort of compensation. And they do so, with increasing frequency.

Doctors may hope this will never come their way but this cannot be ensured—only insured against by membership of a body such as the Medical Protection Society, and this is what Leahy Taylor's excellent book is about. Forewarned, the doctor, surgeon, dentist, or anaesthetist will be on his guard, more careful in his handling of patients, more strict with notes and records, meticulously careful in everything he does, setting the sort of professional standards that will maintain medicine's best repute.

It is time that young doctors—to whom Dr Taylor's book is chiefly directed—had a *vade-mecum* of advice on professional standards, how to handle complaints, allegations of negligence, and the like; how to cooperate with the law and lawyers in the proper demands; where rights end and responsibilities begin. Some are even ill-acquainted with the terms of service they have signed.

Leahy Taylor's long experience of handling such troubles for medical men and women in the Medical Protection Society, and his profound knowledge of the legal intricacies of medical administration and practice, qualify him admirably for this task.

The young doctor will surely find the advice and help this book gives of inestimable value in his dealings with patients, his fellow doctors, and the lawyers whose help he may need. It is a text that is packed with sound practical advice and guidance.

Preface

It has been my endeavour in this second edition to bring up to date that basic knowledge of the law which doctors require for their own protection.

With much pleasure I acknowledge the assistance of my daughter Charlotte Leahy Taylor with the chapter on Courts and Legal Procedure, and others to whom I am indebted include Robert Sumerling, Norman Ellis, my colleague John Fairhurst, my secretary Angela Leaf, and the compiler of the index, my wife.

J.L.T.

Preface
to the First Edition

It is customary, and not without reason, for an author to explain why he has thought it proper to write yet another book to put before the medical student and practitioner. My reason lies in the standpoint from which this book is written. I have not sought to teach the reader how to look after his patients, but rather how to look after himself; not how to get on the Medical Register but how to stay on it.

Many of the troubles in which a doctor may find himself are due to his failure to realise that not everyone has the same high principles as himself, that not every patient he sees can be accepted at his face value, and that it is necessary for his own protection for him to develop a certain degree of caution or, indeed, even of suspicion. When such cases present, adequate knowledge and care will permit the doctor to safeguard as always his patient's interests, yet not to be entirely unmindful of his own.

My thanks are due to many: to the President and Council of the Medical Protection Society for permitting me to refer to cases handled by the Society, and for their encouragement throughout; to Dr Harwood Stevenson, Chairman of Council of the Medical Protection Society for reviewing the text and making many helpful suggestions; to Professor Keith Simpson for whose foreword I am indeed honoured; to my senior colleague and friend, Dr Herbert Constable, whose experience and knowledge have, as always, been most freely available; and to my long-suffering secretaries, Mrs Roberts and Mrs Wale. Lastly, there are those whose misfortunes are referred to herein; doctors who have faced allegations of negligence, of breach of their terms of service or of infamous conduct. These practitioners—many now friends—whom my colleagues and I have been privileged to assist in the darkest days of their professional careers, will, I know, join wholeheartedly with me in the hope that others will learn by precept, rather than as did they, by personal and painful practice.

J.L.T.

1 The Student, the Law, and Registration

Nothing in the status of studentship confers any immunity, either in criminal or civil law. True, a student may be a minor, but the effects upon legal liability and rights result entirely from his 'infancy' and are independent of his being a student. In general, then, a student may be sued in the civil courts and prosecuted in the criminal courts and his occupation affords him no defence. Knowing with what dexterity we all approached our first venu-puncture, appreciating the confidence which attended the first thrust of the trocar and cannula into the hydrocele, and recollecting, still, the prayer which accompanied the lumbar puncture needle on its first, so prolonged, journey, it may seem astonishing that students seldom find themselves defendants in claims for negligence. Let it not be thought that one's early fears were not justified by one's ignorance and hamhandedness. The simple truth is that students have long enjoyed a reputation for impecuniosity. This, whether true in a particular case or not, is sufficient to deter the would-be plaintiff, and his solicitor, mindful of his client's interests, and of his own costs, is likely to suggest the hospital authority as a more worthy target.

Employers have for the employees, and principals for their agents, a liability termed vicarious. It is in consequence of this that a solicitor can turn his client's wrath from the shallow pockets of the student to the deeper coffers of the hospital authority. The authority, of course, will not take this lying down and will cast around to hedge its bet, or, as the legal adviser to the hospital board might express it, to seek indemnity elsewhere. Its eye will likely light upon the consultant in charge of the department where the alleged negligence occurred. He, with a wisdom perhaps acquired by painful experience in younger and more trusting days, will see that the matter lands in the lap of his protection society with the minimum delay.

Not long since, a dental student extracted the wrong tooth and the patient's claim on the hospital authority took the course outlined in the previous paragraph. The Medical Protection Society considered that the consultant's duty was to see that the student was adequately trained and not to require him to do something beyond his knowledge and experience; adequately to instruct him as to what at that moment was required and to supervise him as might be necessary. Beyond this, it was contended, the consultant had no responsibility. Liability for any negligence occurring otherwise lay directly with the student, and vicariously with the hospital authority whose agent the student was. In this case, the student could reasonably be thought competently trained to undertake simple extractions. He had examined the mouth with a registered dental practitioner and seen the record card noting the tooth to be extracted. Should the dental practitioner then have guided the forceps on to the correct tooth? Should the student have been instructed that the extraction must not be commenced until a registered practitioner had confirmed that the forceps were correctly positioned? Was it possible for the practitioner to observe which tooth was being assaulted, or was his view necessarily obstructed by the student's hand? To these apparently simple questions no clear answers can be given, for expert opinions showed only how widely experts can disagree. No criticism of experts is here intended; if they always agreed no cases would require argument, life would lose much of its savour, and the writer might have to seek employment in calmer and less interesting waters.

It will be appreciated that seldom is a medical student the sole or even the essential factor in a case. He works where there are sufficient registered practitioners for one to take over should anything go amiss and, while they will usually save the day, should they fail to do so it is probable that any allegation would be levelled at them rather than at the student. There was, however, the case of Collins *v* Herts C.C.* in which a student acting in wartime as a house officer made an error between cocaine and procaine. The facts, in brief, were that, when taking instructions over the telephone from the surgeon regarding the operating list for the following day, she noted that he would require 100 ml of 1 per cent cocaine with 1 in 20,000 adrenaline. This information she conveyed verbally to the pharmacist who, without query and without requiring a prescription signed by a registered practitioner, made up the solution and sent it to the theatre. It was disputed whether, before injecting the preparation, the surgeon asked the theatre sister whether it was 1 per cent procaine, but in any event about 80 ml were injected, which led of

* (1947) 1 All ER 633.

course to convulsions and death. The Judge found that the surgeon, the house surgeon, and the pharmacist, had all been negligent and divided the damages awarded equally between the surgeon, on the one hand, and the hospital authority (having regard to its vicarious liability for the house surgeon and the pharmacist) on the other.

So, though the student may be at little risk of civil litigation, the possibility exists; he should realise his personal responsibility to use reasonable care and skill and his personal liability should he fail to do so. It follows that he should never, save in real emergency, undertake a procedure without adequate knowledge of the technique, the possible complications, and their treatment. It is easier to ask first than to have to explain later.

Where criminal law is concerned, of course, no vicarious liability exists, and the student is on his own. He should, therefore, be aware of the matters referred to in the chapter on Criminal Law, and especially that part relating to indecent assault. He may find it difficult to secure a chaperon for an examination and his words may be less discreet, and more easily misunderstood, than those of his more experienced colleagues.

The student must not think that examination success alone entitles him to practise his art or craft upon the public. Such privileges as our profession may have are limited to 'registered' practitioners, and it is the act of registration with the General Medical Council which so entitles him. But do not imagine that the privileges to which I refer include any exclusive right to practise medicine. The law of this land confines the practice of veterinary medicine and surgery—with few exceptions—to registered veterinary practitioners, and of dentistry to those on the Dental or Medical Register. But medicine, save in a few specific instances, is a free for all. True, under Section 31 of the Medical Act 1956 a person must not wilfully and falsely hold himself out to be a registered medical practitioner on pain of a fine not exceeding £500, but the difficulty of proving that a person acting in this manner is doing so 'wilfully' has rendered this section largely a dead letter. A number of persons, whose patients certainly believe them to be qualified and registered, have thus escaped prosecution.

The privileges to which registration entitles one will not take long to list. To the registered alone are available medical appointments in hospitals or general practice under the National Health Service Acts, and also appointments in the Armed Forces or the Government Services. No unregistered person may prescribe controlled drugs, sign death or cremation certificates, and a few other less essential documents. Registered practitioners actively engaged in the practice of their profession are exempted from jury service, and, as one who with eminence filled the bench in one of Her Majesty's Coroner's Courts delighted to inform his audience, the newly fledged doctor upon registration ceases to be liable to have his horse commandeered to draw a fire engine. A further privilege which will be retained, unless and until the practitioner inadvertently becomes a Fellow of a Royal College of Physicians, is that of suing for fees.

Registration commenced with the Medical Act of 1858. The General Council for Medical Education and Registration of the United Kingdom was then set up to ensure 'that persons requiring medical aid should be enabled to distinguish qualified from unqualified practitioners'. Since that time an Act of Parliament which speaks of a 'legally qualified' or 'duly qualified' medical practitioner, refers to one on the Medical Register. Of the need for some system to permit the patient to distinguish the qualified from the unqualified in 1858 there can be no doubt. At that time many licensing bodies gave qualifications of widely varying value which entitled the holders to widely varying rights of practice. An Edinburgh graduate was not empowered to practise in Glasgow, and a graduate of the University of London could not practise as a physician in London, where its Royal College of Physicians ran a tightly closed shop. The standards of basic education of those seeking to acquire medical qualifications were often not looked into by the licensing bodies, some of which were undoubtedly of exceedingly easy virtue and must have had a strong attraction for that section of the student body—still, no doubt, with us today—for whom high standards and a low percentage of passes make no very strong appeal. One of the licensing bodies was, indeed, the Archbishop of Canterbury, who last exercised the right to confer the MD Lambeth in 1880. A slight digression here on the history of registration may be of interest; for while many know of the chaotic conditions which existed up to the mid-nineteenth century, few, perhaps, realise that the first moves to register the profession for the benefit of the public were made by the profession itself.

Until several centuries after the Norman Conquest, the Church had a virtual monopoly in all educational matters. But in 1421 a group of physicians petitioned Parliament that the practice of medicine should be confined to those with adequate qualifications. Standards at that time may be judged from part of the preamble which ran, 'In this Realm is every man be he never so lewd taking upon him practice'. Parliament in response gave the King's Council the necessary authority. But these things take time, and little appears to have been done until 1511, when the State first took a hand and decreed that the bishops should, on the advice of examiners, licence medical practitioners. In the city of London, and within seven miles thereof, practice was confined to those licensed by the Bishop of London or the Dean of St Paul's, each of whom were to appoint four examiners. Things then moved with comparative speed, and in 1518, letters patent were issued for the incorporation of physicians in the city; which letters were confirmed by statute four years later, leading to the foundation of the College of Physicians. The requirements then considered necessary were that only persons 'profound, sad, discreet, generally learned and deeply studied in physic' should be licensed.

In 1529, Wolsey's Bull of Legation gave him power to grant licences and doctorates as Legate of the Pope, and by an Act of 1534 the Archbishop of Canterbury was empowered to license practitioners. The attitude of the College of Physicians is shown by the case of Thomas Bonham, an MD of Cambridge who, in 1606, was prosecuted for practising in London, fined £10 and imprisoned pending payment. He succeeded in an action for illegal imprisonment against the President and Censors of the College. Some agreement was eventually reached between Oxford and Cambridge and the College of Physicians, but easily obtained Continental degrees were a recurring difficulty, for these would be incorporated by the universities *ad eundem gradum*.

Bishops, moreover, continued to be authorised to grant licences outside London and, while standards doubtless varied, Hodge's *Vindiciae Medicinae* of 1666 sheds some light on the situation with the couplet:

> 'His money's current and will pass
> Though he who's licensed is an ass'

Registration today, shorn perhaps of some of the eccentricities of earlier times, nevertheless retains its complexities, being of three types, Provisional, Full, and Limited. The essential features of these are as follows:

Provisional Registration

Primary qualification in UK or Republic of Ireland or holding of an overseas qualification recognised by the GMC, and having the necessary knowledge of English.

Limitations on practice: resident house officer in hospital approved for pre-registration service only.

Time limits: none.

Full Registration

Primary qualification in UK or Republic of Ireland, and satisfactory completion of approved resident posts which must include not less than four months in medicine and four months in surgery; or recognised overseas primary qualification and completion of twelve months' satisfactory service as resident house officer in an approved hospital, including four months in medicine and four months in surgery, or other professional experience, acceptable to the GMC, and the necessary knowledge of English; or limited registration with such experience as the GMC may in its discretion accept —at present the guidelines are, qualification for four years, acceptable internship of twelve months, subsequently general clinical experience for twelve months, and two years as registrar or above, at least twelve months of which should be in continuous employment in the UK; or being a national of a member State of the European Economic Community, and holding a primary qualification granted by a Continental member State of the Community; or being an overseas qualified practitioner in the UK temporarily to provide specialist services and accepted for inclusion in the visiting overseas doctors' list; or being included in the list of visiting EEC practitioners.

Limitations on practice: none.

Time limits: none, except in respect of those on the list of visiting EEC practitioners or list of visiting overseas doctors.

Limited Registration

Qualification outside UK acceptable to GMC for purpose of limited registration. Also applicants must have completed outside the UK an acceptable internship of twelve months, or held equivalent appointments. They must also have passed in the UK a test of knowledge of English and of professional knowledge and competence or have been granted exemption by the GMC. They must also satisfy the GMC that they are of good character.

An applicant must have been accepted for employment in an approved hospital in the UK before limited registration can be granted.

Nationals of EEC countries holding qualifications granted in a Continental member State of the EEC do not require to take any test of knowledge of English for registration purposes, though such may be required by prospective employers.

Limitations on practice: practice under the supervision of a fully registered practitioner. Registration may be granted for a specified appointment, or for a specified range of employment within defined dates.

Time limits: five years except in the case of doctors who have had temporary registration in the twelve months prior to February 15 1979 and who first applied for limited registration within an approved period thereafter.

Not all practitioners with limited registration correctly assess their appropriate grade in the hospital hierarchy, and some may apply for posts for which they lack the necessary experience. Consultants sometimes feel moved to inform the GMC that they consider a certain person should only obtain further limited registration in a lower grade. There can be no objection to this in principle, but it should perhaps only be done where there is some unanimity on the point. An obstetric registrar once enquired why her application for further registration had not been approved. Investigation showed that one of the three consultants under whom she had worked had contacted the GMC saying that the applicant was only suitable for a senior house officer appointment. In the face of this the GMC could hardly approve her application. But an approach to the other two consultants resulted in their both contesting their colleague's view, and their statements led the GMC to reverse the previous decision.

Despite the complexity of registration, or perhaps because of it, from time to time some bogus doctor is exposed. Sometimes the identity of an actual doctor has been so well assumed that initial success was highly probable, but too often the deception succeeds for a time owing to lack of what should be routine precaution. Because of the obvious need for such precautions, doctors should appreciate the necessity of their producing evidence of their registration.

Once admitted to the Register an annual fee becomes payable for retention on it. The annual registration certificate provides *prima facie* evidence of registration, and details of registered qualifications, registered address, date of qualifications and registration number can be checked in the Medical Register: the principal list of the 1980 edition contains the names of some 110,000 fully or provisionally registered doctors. The GMC also keeps a register of medical practitioners with limited registration, currently with about 6000 names on it; an overseas list; a visiting overseas doctors list; and a list of visiting EEC practitioners.

Reference to the Medical Register will show the position as it was on January 1 of the year in question. Each fortnight lists are published showing additions, erasures and alterations affecting the principal list. Erasure may be due to transfer to the overseas list, death, disciplinary action, or simply to failure to inform the GMC of a change of address with subsequent failure to pay the annual retention fee. Junior doctors are likely to change their addresses with some frequency, and are therefore well advised to register an address that will ensure that communications from the GMC are received promptly. Resumption of registration attracts a further fee, even if registration had been lost just because the GMC was unable to contact the doctor.

Not surprisingly, in view of the complications of registration, doctors who come to the UK from abroad may on occasion feel that they have been hardly done by when seeking to register with the GMC. The Medical Act of 1978 gave some relief to such feelings by establishing the Review Board for Overseas Qualified Practitioners.

The following classes of doctors may ask the Board to review the GMC decision regarding their registration:

1 Doctors who contend that their overseas qualification, knowledge of English, good character and experience entitle them to full registration.
2 Doctors who contend that their overseas qualification, knowledge of English, and good character entitle them to provisional registration.
3 Doctors who, having held limited registration for not less than three years and six months, have been refused full registration.
4 Doctors whose application for further limited registration has been refused.
5 Doctors erased from the Register of medical practitioners with limited registration on the grounds that they lack the appropriate knowledge and skill.

No right of review is given, however, where the GMC's decision or one of its decisions was that the doctor lacked the necessary experience, did not hold a recognised overseas qualification, or failed to demonstrate a satisfactory knowledge of English.

The doctor then who feels that he has a case in accordance with the rules as outlined above can require the Registrar of the GMC to give a reason in writing for the GMC's decision, and then apply for review of that decision by the Board. Should the Chairman of the Board decide that an oral hearing is necessary, the doctor may attend and may be represented or assisted by a doctor or lawyer.

2 Employers

Until the day the student qualifies, his life has been largely under the control of others. They have, according to their lights, if not always according to his, no doubt acted with his best interest in mind. From the day he qualifies, his life is largely under the control of those to whom his interests are of secondary importance. The interests of most newly qualified doctors are adequately looked after by their immediate employers within the limits of their powers but exceptions undoubtedly occur. The first essential is that the doctor should have some understanding of the authorities under which he works.

At the time of writing the National Health Service is about to undergo one of its periodical administrative reshuffles and some of the details are yet to be filled in. The essential structure is however now clear.

At the top of the pyramid are the Secretaries of State responsible for the Department of Health, the Scottish Home and Health Department, and the Welsh and Northern Ireland offices. Then in England come the 14 Regional Health Authorities, and with the forthcoming abolition of the tier of Area Health Authorities we drop to the District Health Authorities, the employers of the junior doctor. In Wales there are 8 Health Authorities divided into districts, in Scotland 15 Health Boards similarly divided into districts, and in Northern Ireland below the Department of Health and Social Services are the 4 Health and Social Services Boards.

The Regional Health Authority is responsible for the coordination for the Service, resources allocation, determining the extent and distribution of specialised facilities, including facilities for undergraduate medical education, major capital building projects, liaison with universities, and the implementation of Government policies.

The Chairman and other members of an RHA are appointed by the Secretary of State following consultation with the university in the area, Health Authorities, organisations representing the profession and other interests.

The District Health Authorities—each one will have a name appropriate to the district it serves—will total almost 200, and will consist of a Chairman appointed by the Secretary of State and 15 other members appointed by the Regional Health Authority. The membership will include 1 hospital consultant, 1 general practitioner, 1 nurse/midwife or health visitor, a nominee of the appropriate university with a medical school in the region, a member recommended by the trade union movement, 4 members appointed by local authorities and generalist members to bring the total membership to 16.

The District Health Authorities are responsible for the planning, development and management of health services in their respective districts within national and regional guidelines. This will include responsibility for primary care, general hospital services, maternity and child welfare services, services for the elderly and mentally ill, and for the mentally handicapped. Consultation machinery will be established with local health authorities, community health councils and bodies representing the various professions employed in the health services.

Under the District Health Authority will be a District Management Team, composed of four officers of the DHA, namely a community physician, a nurse, the treasurer, and an administrator, together with two clinical representatives, one a hospital consultant and one a general practitioner. It is the function of the DMT to advise the District Health Authority, both generally and specifically, on the current and anticipated needs of the Service and to give opinions as to relevant priorities.

The District Health Authority will have discretion as to how it exerts its management function in different hospitals or groups of hospitals. There will be for each unit of management an administrator, and a director of nursing services, but otherwise there may be much variation under different DHAs. A District Hospital Medical Committee will be required and, in the larger districts at least, Medical Executive Committees. The appropriate medical committee would, it is anticipated, be required to send a representative to the unit group of management.

The other type of medical committee is that representative of a specialty, and where these are continued under the new administration their views will probably be passed to the District Hospital Medical Committee.

To return to the administrative structure, the essential and very apparent feature of the organisation is the absolute and complete control over appointments held by the Secretary of State. Under this hierarchy, the doctor is employed as a servant of his employing authority. Before looking at the specific regulations which bind him, it will be as well to give some consideration to the master/servant relationship, and to the implications of his working and residing in his employer's property as determined by the Occupiers' Liability Act 1957.

Master and Servant

Employment Legislation

Legislation regarding employment has become a legal jungle of recent years and all that is attempted here is the barest outline of the employee's rights and duties under the relevant Acts.

Trade Union and Labour Relations Act 1974
Trade Union and Labour Relations (Amendment) Act 1976
Under these Acts an employee has a right not to be unfairly dismissed.

Dismissal is fair if it is necessitated by the employee's lack of ability, his conduct or by redundancy; if with certain safeguards the employee is on strike or for other substantial reason.

Dismissal is unfair if it results from the employee exercising his right to belong to a union and take part in its activities at an appropriate time; from redundancy where the effect was not applied equally to all employees; or from striking if others taking part were not also dismissed.

These provisions regarding unfair dismissal do not apply where the employment has lasted for less than 52 weeks, to part-timers working less than 21 hours a week, or to those over normal retiring age.

An important consideration is that an employee may be treated as having been dismissed even if he has resigned, if he can show that his resignation was brought about by his employer's conduct.

Complaints of unfair dismissal, should the conciliation officer fail to settle them, come before an industrial tribunal. If the complainant is successful the tribunal may recommend reinstatement in the same position, re-engagement in another position or award compensation.

The complainant has a duty to mitigate his loss, e.g. by seeking alternative employment, and an appeal procedure is available against the tribunal's decision.

Health and Safety at Work Act 1974

This Act is aimed at protecting the health and safety of people whilst at work, protecting the public from risk arising from work, and controlling the use of dangerous and noxious substances.

These functions are carried out by the Health and Safety Commission through the Health and Safety Executive. The Employment Medical Advisory Service is the medical branch of the Executive.

Employers have a duty to safeguard the health and safety of their employees by providing 'so far as reasonably practical', safe plant, safe systems of work, safety training and supervision, and safe access and egress. Employees should be provided with a statement of the employer's health and safety policy.

Employees are required to exercise reasonable care for their own health and safety and for the health and safety of others. Trade unions appoint safety representatives whom employers are required to consult.

Health and safety inspectors have the right to inspect premises and to require information, and they are entitled to serve 'improvement notices' where they consider that statutory provisions are not being complied with and 'prohibition' notices forbidding continuation of unsafe activities. These notices can be appealed against, but should they be ignored legal proceedings may be instituted.

Sex Discrimination Act 1975

This Act distinguishes between direct and indirect discrimination. The former is the giving of clear preference as by advertising for male applicants only, and the latter the making of conditions which in effect limit applicants to one sex or other. Similarly direct and indirect discretion can occur where married and single people are accorded different treatment. Discrimination is lawful when, and only when, the sex is a 'genuine occupational qualification'. It is not only in the selection of candidates for a position that sexual discrimination is unlawful, but in all other aspects of employment such as training and promotion.

The Equal Opportunities Commission may assist those who believe they have been discriminated against, and Legal Aid is also available.

Complaints are made to a tribunal. A conciliation officer may endeavour to achieve a settlement, but failing this the tribunal comes to its decision. A successful complainant may receive compensation up to a fixed limit in respect of losses incurred, together with damages for injured feelings. The employer may also be required to take specific action.

Race Relations Act 1976

This Act runs parallel with the Sex Discrimination Act 1975. The Commission for Racial Equality fulfils the same function as the Equal Opportunities Commission; direct and indirect discrimination is recognised and discrimination is lawful where there exists a 'genuine occupational qualification'.

Legal Aid is available to complainants, and complaints may be made to a tribunal. A conciliation officer may endeavour to achieve a settlement, and the tribunal when satisfied that there has been unlawful discrimination will declare the rights of the parties, award compensation, and recommend action to eliminate discrimination. The compensation which may be awarded is subject to a fixed limit, and apart from losses incurred, injured feelings are also taken into account.

Employment Protection Act 1975

This Act set up the Advisory, Conciliation and Arbitration Service, the function of which is to seek to improve industrial relations and to seek to settle disputes by conciliation or arbitration.

Also established were the Central Arbitration Committee which deals with matters referred to it by ACAS, and the Employment Appeals Tribunal which hears appeals from industrial tribunals.

Employees suspended on the grounds of risks to health or safety are entitled to full pay up to 26 weeks provided they have completed 4 weeks' service, are fit and available for work and have not unreasonably refused alternative work.

Maternity leave entitlement as laid down by this Act does not directly affect the doctor in the hospital service of the NHS as the matter is covered in her Terms and Conditions of Service (see page 27).

Provisions are made to permit employees who are JPs, members of local authorities, statutory tribunals, health authorities, educational authorities and water boards to have reasonable time off without pay.

The unfair dismissal rules are amended to bring in employees working 16 hours a week, and after 5 years' service, those working 8 hours a week.

Where the tribunal is deciding on reinstatement or re-engagement it will take into consideration the employee's wishes, the practicability to the employer, whether the employee contributed to his dismissal, and the reasonableness of the employer's action if he had engaged a permanent replacement.

An employer who unreasonably refuses an order to reinstate or re-engage an employee is required to make an additional payment to him which ranges between 13 and 52 weeks' pay with an upper limit on a 'week's pay'.

The usual award is, however, composed of a basic and a compensatory award. The basic award ranges between 2 and 30 weeks' pay, and the compensatory award is such amount as the tribunal considers fair having regard to the loss the employee had sustained as a result of his dismissal. Both awards have upper limits which are reassessed annually.

An employee is entitled to a written statement of the reasons for his dismissal on request.

The regulations regarding redundancy in the Act have little relevance to the doctor as the matter is dealt with in his Terms and Conditions of Service.

The Act amends the Contracts of Employment Act 1972 with the effect that statements must be given to employees working not less than 16 hours per week, or after 5 years not less than 8 hours per week. The statement must contain the job title, the disciplinary rules or a reference to a document containing them, and the period of notice required subject to a statutory minimum.

Employees are entitled to an itemised pay statement, and those on fixed term contracts—except contracts of 12 weeks or less—are covered by the provisions of the Act.

Employment Protection (Consolidation) Act 1978

This Act consolidates much previous legislation, notably the Factories Act 1961, the Offices Shops and Railway Premises Act 1963, the Redundancy Payments Act 1965, the Contracts of Employment Act 1972, and the Rehabilitation of Offenders Act 1974.

Under this Act, as previously under the Contracts of Employment Act 1972, employers are required to provide employees, within 13 weeks of their commencing service, with a statement setting out the essentials of the post. These include the title of the job, rates of pay, hours of work, holiday entitlement, periods of notice, pension details, grievance procedures, and disciplinary rules with rights of appeal. These particulars may be provided by reference to some available document.

There are statutory minimum notice periods—one week either way after four weeks' service, and after two years' service the employer must give not less than one week for each year's service up to twelve weeks for twelve years and over.

The provisions regarding redundancy, formerly the Redundancy Payments Act 1975, provide for lump sum payments in the event of redundancy depending on length of service, with certain exclusions such as a minimum period of service and a minimum number of hours worked per week.

The relevance of the provisions regarding the Rehabilitation of Offenders—formerly the Rehabilitation of Offenders Act 1974—is simply that the provisions for wiping the slate clean do not apply to medical practitioners or to certain other professional groups.

Employment Act 1980

Under this Act unfair dismissal rights may be excluded in fixed term contracts of one year or more, basic awards for unfair dismissal may be reduced where the employee's general conduct so merits, or where the employee has unreasonably refused an offer of re-employment. The minimum basic award of two weeks' sick pay also ceases to exist.

Apart from the legislation, there are then some general considerations of the master and servant relationship.

Difficulty may arise in circumstances thought to justify immediate suspension or dismissal. Disciplinary procedures will be dealt with when considering the relevant regulations, but circumstances can arise casting reasonable doubt on a doctor's fitness to occupy his post or fulfil his duties. For example, a charge may be pending concerning an alleged act of indecency or misuse of drugs. It cannot be thought that a hospital authority would be acting improperly were it to suspend a doctor in such circumstances while awaiting the hearing, although, in general, such suspension should be on full pay. Acts of disobedience such as refusal to see a patient when so instructed may also warrant immediate suspension and, in some cases, immediate dismissal. Not uncommonly, disputes may hinge upon the duty of a particular doctor to see a particular patient. If the doctor does not consider it to be his duty he may certainly put his view to his superior. But if he is then told to attend to the patient he should do so, and later pursue the question of the limitations of his duty if he be so minded. Irrespective of any rights to a period of notice, there exists a common law right of either party to consider a contract terminated where such a view is justified by the conduct of the other. A doctor who, for example, leaves the hospital where he is employed without permission cannot expect to be entitled to return and resume duty some days later. The hospital may reasonably claim that the contract has been terminated by the doctor's conduct.

Illness, as a general rule, does not provide reasonable cause for instant dismissal. Indeed, where the doctor is entitled to a certain period of sick leave, one would not anticipate that notice would be given until that period had come to an end. It could be, however, that a locum if ill might reasonably be held unable to fulfil any substantial part of his engagement. Instant dismissal could then be justified.

Property of Servant

Not uncommonly, a resident doctor contacts the Medical Protection Society concerning property missing from his room in the hospital. He is anxious to know whether he has a claim against his employers. The answer, unfortunately, is 'no'. Employers are not the insurers of their servants' goods, and the fact that a doctor may be compulsorily resident does not alter this position. This was determined in the case of Edwards *v* West Herts Group Hospital Management Committee*. The Court of Appeal held that no duty of care was owed by the Hospital Management Committee to the plaintiff houseman. The claim was in negligence, and negligence is a tort which consists of a failure to exercise a duty of care. It follows that where there is no such duty there can be no negligence. The circumstances were that Edwards, a compulsorily resident houseman, occupied hospital accommodation for which a fixed sum was deducted from his remuneration. Goods were stolen from his room, and the Court did not accept that there was any term implied in the contract to the effect that the employing authority would take reasonable care of its servants' property. The severity of the law in this matter has been to some extent mitigated by Circular HM(56)31, which lays down that hospital authorities should warn their staff that no responsibility is accepted and advise them to seek insurance cover. The authority is also empowered to make *ex gratia* payments under certain circumstances. This may be done where the loss or damage occurs in working quarters not used exclusively by the staff, the articles concerned are such as might reasonably be carried in working

* (1975) 1 WLR. 415.

quarters, and where there has been no negligence by the employee. Payment may alternatively be made where the owner has no insurance cover, and the loss or damage arises from the negligence of the hospital authority or the inadequacy of cloakroom facilities.

Injury to Employee

At common law, an employer is liable for injury to his employee arising from the negligence of the employer himself or from that of a fellow employee. Should it be that the injured employee has been guilty of contributory negligence, this will tend to lessen the damages awarded but will not bar his claim.

The possibility of injury by mentally afflicted patients is a risk to which doctors, in common with other members of hospital staff, are particularly exposed. No court decision can be quoted on the probable liability of the patient in respect of injury suffered by a doctor, but it is thought that, insofar as the action of the patient results from the condition for the treatment of which he is in the hospital, the doctor, in undertaking that treatment, would be held to have willingly accepted the risk involved. Whether the hospital authority would be liable would depend upon the circumstances. In the case of Mitchie *v* Shenley and Napsbury Hospital Management Committee* it was held that the Hospital Management Committee was not liable in respect of the injuries suffered by the plaintiff, a nurse, who had been attacked by a patient. The Court considered that there had been no negligence by the Hospital Management Committee and that the plaintiff, knowing that the patient might be violent, had not taken appropriate precautions such as seeking assistance. Like any other employing body, however, a hospital authority is obliged to take reasonable precautions for the safety of its employees, and should there be failure in this respect (e.g. by inadequate staffing or failure to warn new staff of a patient's aggressive tendencies where these are exceptional), then the employee might have an action in negligence were he to suffer damage.

Before leaving the subject of injury, it may be helpful to summarise the possible rights of an injured employee in the Health Service. These are:

1 Sick pay for a period dependent on the length of service.

* *The Times*, 19 March 1953.

2 Industrial injuries benefit, where an accident has occurred at work, or the claimant is suffering from a Scheduled Disease. Tuberculosis is such a disease in the case of those employed in the treatment of tuberculosis, in research laboratories, or post-mortem work concerned with this disease.
3 Superannuation benefits in the case of those permanently disabled.
4 Claims against the employer, e.g. in negligence or under the Occupiers' Liability Act.

Occupiers' Liability Act

Apart from being the doctor's master, the hospital authority is also the occupier of the property, i.e. the hospital in which the doctor works, and as such has responsibilities to him under the Occupiers' Liability Act 1957. By this Act the occupier owes a 'common duty of care' to all 'visitors', which term, surprisingly perhaps, includes employees, and indeed all persons legally on the premises. Since the coming into operation of this Act there has no longer been a distinction between invitees and licensees, and no longer does a warning discharge an occupier's duty, unless such warning is adequate to render the visitor 'reasonably safe'. One clause which might in certain circumstances bar a doctor's claim against his employer, is that which states that an occupier may expect that a person in the exercise of his calling will appreciate and guard against any special risk incidental to it so far as the occupier leaves him free to do so. Another clause frees the occupier from any liability in respect of injury resulting from a risk willingly accepted by the visitor.

Two examples of claims by doctors against their employing authority under this Act must suffice. In the first, a doctor slipped on a floor which was thick with polish, sustaining serious injury. It was not until some derisory offers had been rejected and legal proceedings were in contemplation that a satisfactory offer was put forward. There appeared to be no doubt that there was nothing in the way of a warning which would have made the doctor reasonably safe, nor was the risk willingly undertaken as there was no alternative to traversing that particular area of floor.

In the second case, a doctor parked his car in a place where doctors habitually did so, though no particular parking places were marked out at the hospital in question. A piece of masonry fell from the building damaging the car, and the question of the hospital authority's liability arose. This is not the place to go into the liability of the authority *vis-à-vis* that of the independent contractors who had recently carried out work on the building, and in due course the doctor's repair bill was paid by the hospital authority.

Terms and Conditions of Service

In April 1981 was published the latest edition of Hospital Medical and Dental Staff (England and Wales) Terms and Conditions of Service. This together with the General Whitley Council Conditions of Service—which deals with employees other than doctors and dentists—puts flesh and blood around the bare bones of the contract of employment.

Before touching on a number of matters dealt with in the Terms and Conditions of Service, a few general points. Some issues are left to the discretion of the employing authorities. Thus, when the word 'may', or similar, appears, it is advisable to proceed discreetly, to request consideration, not to clamour about one's rights. Secondly, the NHS is by and large a good employer. The provisions of employment compare favourably with the vast majority of those available in the private sector and in other occupations of comparable level. Petty irritations and occasional injustices occur, but the favourable overall picture should not be lost sight of and it is often advisable to take a long term view when disagreements arise.

There are also certain expenses and fees that can be claimed. Doctors are trusted to deal with these honestly, and overclaiming, whether by carelessness or by fraud, is apt to be dealt with severely. There can be no complaint about this, but it is tragic indeed when a doctor's career is wrecked over such an issue. It is therefore worth stressing the need for complete accuracy in submitting such claims.

In general, then, what should be done if one thinks that one is not getting a fair deal? A copy of the Terms and Conditions of Service should be provided for all hospital doctors, and it is often helpful to ask the hospital administrator to explain in writing the reason for his views. If the feelings of injustice persist the first person to consult in most cases is the POWAR—the BMA's Place of Work Accredited Representative. He sometimes, with help from the Industrial Relations Officer—another BMA official—will be able to solve or at least explain the majority of problems. Sometimes—as often with substandard accommodation—it is one's successor who will benefit; but then, have we not all some reason to be grateful for the efforts of our predecessors?

If legal issues arise at any stage or if disciplinary action is threatened, then the doctor's protection society should be immediately notified and the matter left in its hands.

A brief look then at some of the Terms and Conditions of Service.

Pay. Rates of pay are recommended each year by the Independent Review Body and may be reduced, phased or otherwise interfered with by the government of the day as political expediency dictates. The standard working week for senior registrars, senior house officers and house officers is a minimum of ten units of medical time, each unit being of four hours' duration.

For additional units of medical time further payments are made. Each class A unit—standing by or working in hospitals—attracts payment at the rate of 30 per cent of 1/10th of a week's basic salary, and class B units—available on call—1/3rd of the class A rate.

A doctor, although at home, may qualify for class A units where he is fully on standby as if he were in the hospital.

Remunerable time is assessed as a weekly average taking into account the normal duty roster, any commitments outside such duties and such cover for colleagues on annual and study leave as may be contracted. Subject to patient need there should be a minimum period of 88 hours per week off duty.

Tenure of Post. The grades of consultant, associate specialist and hospital practitioner are career grades and may be retained until retirement. Appointments in the grade of senior registrar, registrar, senior house officer, and house officer are usually held for four years, two or three years, one year and six months respectively. Some appointments are subject to confirmation after an initial period, usually of one year.

Retention of Other Fees. Doctors are entitled to undertake other work which does not in the opinion of the employing authority interfere with contracted duties. Where hospital laboratory or X-ray facilities are used, 1/3rd of the fees earned are payable to the hospital authority.

It is not always easy to determine for which services fees can be charged, and the Terms and Conditions of Service list as category I items, those coming within the doctor's contractual duties, and as category II, those outside such duties, for which a charge may be made. A list cannot be exhaustive and should be regarded as laying down guiding principles.

The item which causes most difficulty in practice is the report requested by the patient or, with the patient's consent, by an interested third party. If the patient is under observation or treatment at the hospital and the information requested can be given without a separate examination and without an appreciable amount of work in extracting information from casenotes, then it comes in category I and no fee is chargeable. If the patient is no longer attending hospital or should a special examination or an appreciable amount of work in extracting information be required, then category II becomes appropriate.

Other matters that come under category I include:

a Examination and reporting on patients referred by doctors who, having examined the patient, require a second opinion, e.g. patients referred by GPs, Service MOs, community or occupational health physicians.
b Examination and reporting for prophylactic purposes as agreed between the Secretary of State and the profession, e.g. investigation of contacts of transmissible diseases, exclusion of transmissible diseases in teachers and employees of health and local authorities who are at risk of acquiring or spreading such diseases by reason of their employment, screening procedures for approved groups, the majority of recommendations under the Mental Health Act, and attendance at Court hearings as a witness to fact where a doctor is giving evidence on his own behalf or on behalf of his employing authority in a case in which he is professionally concerned.

The more common types of case coming under category II, after that already mentioned, include examination and reports in connection with insurance, superannuation, foreign travel, emigration, sport and recreation, provided that such examinations are not concerned with diagnosis and treatment of injuries or accidents.

Reports for coroners and attendances at Coroners' Courts are category II work, as are examinations and reports in connection with legal actions, other than those already referred to as category I. Both cremation certificates—Certificate B and Certificate C—attract a fee.

When doubt or difficulty arises the Terms and Conditions of Service should be consulted and advice sought before any claim is made.

Private Practice

Doctors in the hospital service may undertake private practice subject to the requirement that those in grades other than consultant may undertake it only outside the time for which they are contracted to an employing authority. Provisionally registered doctors are of course limited to the duties of their post, and those with limited or conditional registration, to the precise terms of their registration certificate.

Whole-time doctors must not exceed 10 per cent of their gross salary from their private practice, and should consultants or associate specialists do so for two consecutive years, their contract will be deemed to be one of maximum part-time which will have the effect of reducing the salary by 1/11th.

Part-time Appointments

Senior registrars, registrars, senior house officers and house officers may contract for less than ten units of medical time per week, with additional units at Class A or Class B rates. Remuneration is at the rate of 1/10th of the appropriate weekly salary for each standard unit of medical time. In the case of consultants, associate specialists and hospital practitioners—who are by definition GP principals—the hospital authority assesses the average time taken to perform the duties of the post and expresses this as notional half days, each of which is regarded as being of 3½ hours' duration. Travelling time is calculated at a maximum of half an hour each way.

Cover during Absences

In general, doctors are expected to deputise for absent colleagues even though it involves interchange of staff between hospitals.

Deputising is not of course always practicable, and in such cases it is the doctor's responsibility to inform the hospital authority of the need for a locum. The duty of providing that locum lies with the authority and not with the doctor.

The cover foreseeably necessary in respect of annual and study leave should be taken account of in the doctor's job description. Cover for short spells of sickness during the standard working day may properly be required, as may additional duties in occasional emergencies. Doctors are permitted to act as locums in their own hospitals, though not of course within the hours for which they are already contracted.

Concern is often expressed about the danger to patients resulting from doctors being required to work excessive hours. The regulations state that a doctor on a one in two rota is not required to contract to cover a colleague's absence on annual or study leave. Where, however, in such circumstances a locum from outside cannot be obtained, there is no option but to seek cover from a member of the hospital staff.

Locums

Locums in the grades of senior registrar, registrar, senior house officer or house officer are engaged for the standard working week contract for ten units of medical time at the standard rate, together with any additional Class A or Class B units.

Where the doctor accepts a locum appointment in his own hospital he contracts for each unit of medical time required at 1/10th of the standard rate.

An acting up allowance is payable to a doctor taking over, with the employing authority's approval, the full duties of a doctor in a senior grade. This provision normally relates to a doctor acting in the absence of a consultant and only exceptionally to acting up in lower grades.

Starting Salaries and Incremental Dates

In general a doctor is appointed to the minimum point on the scale for the appropriate grade and his incremental date is the date on which he takes up his appointment.

Where, however, in a regular appointment the doctor has previously served in the same or in a higher grade, such previous service is with few exceptions counted in full in determining his starting salary and incremental dates.

Following regular service in the same or in a higher grade, subsequent locum service counts in full towards incremental credit. In other cases locum service of three months or more counts towards incremental credit at the rate of a half on regular appointment to that grade. Service outside the NHS may be taken into account in determining starting salaries. Senior registrars who on appointment have spent more than three years in the registrar grade and registrars who have spent more than two years as an SHO are entitled to extra increments.

Protection of Salary

A provision which causes a deal of difficulty is that whereby a doctor taking an appointment in a lower grade which is recognised by the authority as being for the purpose of obtaining approved training, may retain the salary he received in his previous appointment. The crucial point is that the post should be for approved training purposes. Such approval should be sought before the post is accepted. Hospital authorities vary in their interpretation, but in general, taking a job to which one needs to obtain full registration or enables one to sit an examination is not seen as an approved training purpose. Should the doctor's consultant advise that a period be spent in some other branch of the speciality, then approval by the hospital authority can reasonably be anticipated.

Residents' Charges

Doctors required as a condition of their appointment to live in a hospital, or to stay there overnight on one night in three or more often, are entitled to free accommodation. Should, however, such a doctor elect to live in a hospital house or apartment for which a rental charge is appropriate, then abatement from that rental will be made. Doctors who voluntarily live in the hospital are charged appropriately for their accommodation. Non-resident doctors required to stay in the hospital overnight on duty regularly but less often than one night in three are charged proportionately. No charge may be made when a doctor with no regular commitment to do so is required to stay overnight.

Where the accommodation or the furnishings are below standard the charges may be reduced. Lodging charges are calculated on the assumption that the doctor will be away during his annual leave. Should he be permitted to remain in residence a further charge at the same rate as the charge already made will also be deducted from his salary.

No charge is made after the first week of sick leave if the doctor is an in-patient or away from the hospital; similarly, when absent on study leave or official leave without subsistence expenses. Charges are made for all meals taken in the hospital.

Termination of Employment

House officers are entitled to receive and required to give two weeks' notice; senior house officers, one month; registrars, two months' senior registrars, associate specialists and consultants, three months'. This does not, of course, prevent both parties to the contract agreeing to a different period nor to payment being made in lieu of notice.

Whilst these provisions cover the vast majority of cases, there is of course a standard of conduct which permits an employer to dismiss any employee without notice.

It sometimes happens that a doctor wishes to leave his post without giving the required period of notice, or indeed, having accepted a post, does not wish to take it up. The usual situation is that a better job has unexpectedly turned up and will be lost unless accepted without delay.

In such circumstances it is perfectly reasonable for the doctor to ask to be released from his contract. He can reasonably expect that the employing authority would look sympathetically at his request provided a replacement can be found and patient care is not jeopardised. A contract is, however, a contract. The doctor would be rightly aggrieved if the authority failed to keep its side of the bargain, and the authority can reasonably expect no less of the doctor. The fact that the authority is very unlikely to sue for breach of contract is irrelevant. The doctor who ignores his contractual obligations in this way may find himself reported to the GMC, and he can hardly complain if information is passed from one employing authority to another and future jobs are found hard to come by.

Annual Leave

Consultants, associate specialists after two years' service, and senior registrars are entitled to six weeks' leave per year; other associate specialists, registrars and senior house officers to five weeks'. House officers are entitled to four weeks', to be taken during the occupancy of the post and not carried forward to subsequent appointments. There is also an entitlement to ten days' statutory and public holidays or days in lieu. Doctors should notify their employing authority when they wish to take leave and the granting of leave is subject to adequate arrangements being made to cover their work. It follows that the longer the notice given, the more likely that the response will be favourable.

Sick Leave

Entitlement to sick pay is dependent on length of service, ranging from one month's full pay, and, after four months' service, two months' half pay during the first year, to six months' full and six months' half pay after five years' service. Adjustments are made in respect of benefits received under Social Security Acts and certain other payments with a view to ensuring that the total being received does not exceed normal salary. It is laid down that doctors should immediately notify their employing authority when ill, should submit doctors' statements as required, and in particular on admission to and discharge from hosptial. There is a strange reluctance on the part of doctors to seek medical certificates, yet they should know better than others that they are seldom offered unless requested.

Study Leave

Study leave should be granted up to the recommended standards provided that essential services can be maintained. The recommended standards are, for a consultant or associate specialist, 30 days including days off duty falling within the leave period, in a period of 3 years; for a senior registrar at least 1 day per week plus 30 days in 3 years; and for a registrar, senior house officer and post-registration house officer, 1 day per week within university terms, or a maximum of 30 days per year. Further leave may be granted for sitting for higher examinations. Doctors will normally receive pay and expenses when taking such study leave, and when on paid leave no remunerative work may be undertaken without the authority's express permission.

Pre-registration house officers have no entitlement to study leave as such, but should be allowed time within working hours for attending conferences and rounds within the hospital.

Employing authorities have discretion to allow further periods of study leave in appropriate circumstances.

Maternity Leave

Entitlement to maternity leave with pay is dependent upon having been employed by a health or local authority for 12 months without a break in service of more than 3 months at the beginning of the eleventh week before the expected week of confinement.

Application should be made as early as possible and must be made not later than 21 days before the commencement of the leave, which is normally immediately before the beginning of the eleventh week before the expected week of confinement. A further requirement is that the doctor should state in writing her intention to continue in the Health Service for at least 3 months after completion of her leave. Those who cannot meet these requirements are entitled to unpaid leave for a similar period. The commencement of maternity leave may be postponed on production of an appropriate medical certificate.

The leave period is one of up to 18 weeks commencing not less than 11 weeks before the expected date of confinement, though the post-natal period is reduced to 1 month should the child not live. There is, however, a statutory right to return to work up to 29 weeks after confinement, but time taken after the 18 weeks will be without pay and the employing authority must be given at least 21 days' notice of this intention.

Pay during maternity leave varies from full pay for the first 4 weeks to half pay at the end. Deductions are made in respect of sickness benefit and allowances to ensure that full pay is not exceeded. Should a doctor fail to return to work having undertaken to do so, a refund may be required.

Expenses

The first point to stress is that expenses are paid for the purpose of reimbursement only. If the money for which the claim is made has not, for any reason whatever, been spent, the claim is fraudulent, and if the fraud is detected prosecution will likely follow. Secondly, claims should be submitted as soon as possible, and if unduly delayed difficulties in payment may arise.

Travelling Expenses

It is not proposed here to go into the complexity of travelling expenses. The principles are three-fold. Mileage allowances are payable for journeys undertaken on behalf of the employing authority. No allowance is normally payable for the usual daily journey between home and hospital. Special arrangements apply in respect to home to hospital mileage when the car is required that day for an official journey.

Depending on the amount of use of the vehicle, payment will be made at the standard rate or the regular user rate. Subject to certain conditions, regular users with a high mileage on duty may be allocated a Crown car, or provided with a loan at favourable rates for car purchase.

Removal Expenses

The fundamental requirement is that, prior to expenses being reimbursed and grants paid, the employing authority must be satisfied that the removal of the doctor's home is required and that the arrangements proposed are satisfactory. This condition being complied with, removal expenses are paid in full in the following circumstances:

1 A whole-time practitioner required to move, without changing his headquarters hospital, into or out of hospital accommodation which he was or is required to occupy as part of his terms of service.
2 Senior house officers, registrars and senior registrars who transfer on the expiry of their appointment to full-time posts in these grades.
3 Doctors taking up whole-time first appointments as consultant or associate specialist or full-time posts as senior registrar, registrar or senior house officer having previously been in posts approved for this purpose.
4 Consultants moving in the interests of the service.

Special arrangements apply to rotational appointments and for long term locums.

The expenses which can be claimed include the contractor's charges for the move—three tenders required—storage as necessary, legal fees, stamp duty, survey fees, interest on bridging loans where approved, estate agents' fees, costs of a preliminary visit, losses on season tickets, school fees, etc. There is also a miscellaneous expenses grant which covers any additional expenses incurred.

The regulations are complex and should be read in detail prior to a move. The essential requirements in practice are that the doctor acts reasonably, which in essence means that he incurs only such expenses as he would incur were he himself footing the bill, and where doubts arise it is but common sense to seek the agreement of the employing authority before incurring the debt.

Should the move result in increased payments in respect of rates and property insurance, a so-called excess rent allowance may be claimed, and again the up-to-date regulations should be consulted.

House Purchase

Advances of salary to assist with house purchase may be made in defined circumstances.

Procedure for Settling Differences

A doctor dissatisfied with an item of his Terms and Conditions of Service, other than dismissal or disciplinary action, has a right of appeal to his employing authority and to appear before that authority, with, if desired, a representative of his union or professional association. Should the doctor remain aggrieved following such appeal, a further appeal to the Regional Appeals Committee can be made by the BMA.

The function of a Regional Appeals Committee is to ensure that national conditions of service are applied locally. It consists of an equal number of management and staff, and at the hearing the doctor's case is put by the BMA's representative. Should the Committee fail to reach a decision, the matter may be referred by either party to the appropriate council of the Whitley Councils for the Health Service.

Disciplinary Action

Disciplinary action can be taken by an employing authority against a hospital doctor on three distinct counts; personal conduct, professional conduct and professional competence. So far as personal conduct is concerned, doctors are in precisely the same position as other members of the staff and governed by the same regulations. These permit employing authorities to delegate the power of dismissal to an individual or committee of the authority in the case of junior staff, while those holding senior appointments may only be dismissed therefrom by a decision of the full employing authority. There should be a proper warning of possible disciplinary action whenever possible, the doctor should have the right to be heard in his own defence, and an appeal body should be appointed from the employing authority before which the doctor can appear in person, or with a representative of his protection organisation. Legal representation is not permitted, and the appeal committee should not include any person directly involved in the circumstances leading to the disciplinary action or persons who were members of any committee which orginally recommended the dismissal. These requirements provide no more than is necessary to see that justice is done, but it is still not unknown for hospital authorities to dismiss summarily a resident entirely without regard to the elements of natural justice. The classical case was that of Palmer*, a house officer who was one day informed by a deputy medical superintendent that, in view of certain incidents, it had been decided to dismiss him. He was paid up until two days later and the following day, a Christmas Day as it happened, he was bodily removed from the premises. Palmer appealed to the employing authority who appointed a committee which, in due course, reported that its unanimous opinion was that the dismissal was unjustified. The board considered the report of the committee in the presence of the medical superintendent, deputy medical superintendent, and the legal adviser, and on the casting vote of the Chairman decided that the dismissal was justified. The matter was then taken into court where Palmer was successful. It was held that for the board to have allowed the presence of the medical superintendent, his deputy, and the legal adviser when Palmer was not given equal facilities was contrary to natural justice. The hospital authority in this case put up the somewhat surprising defence that the disciplinary regulations were advisory and not obligatory. But it was held that they were indeed incorporated in the contract of service.

In cases concerning professional conduct or professional competence, it is for the Chairman of the appointing authority to determine whether there is a *prima facie* case which could result in serious disciplinary action. Any preliminary enquiries necessary to assist the Chairman in reaching his decision are dealt with by the regional or district medical officer on behalf of a regional or district health authority, or the secretary on behalf of a board of governors. Therefore, where a doctor is instructed to report to any of these authorities, it is essential that he determines precisely what the purpose of the interview is, and in most cases he would be well advised to seek advice before making any statement. Unless the Chairman decides that no *prima facie* case exists, the doctor should be informed in writing of the allegation or complaint, and told that

* Palmer *v* Inverness Hospitals Board of Management (1963) SLT 124.

an enquiry is under consideration. He should be given time to take advice and make representations before the final decision is taken on whether an enquiry is necessary.

Should the Chairman decide that there is a *prima facie* case, and that there is a dispute as to the facts, an enquiry is set up, but should the facts be agreed, the procedure is as for cases of personal conduct. The composition of the enquiry panel is obviously of importance, and it is laid down that no member should be associated with the hospital in question, and the usual panel consists of three persons with a legally qualified Chairman. Regard is also to be had, in cases concerning professional competence, to the advisability of appointing a person in the same specialty, and possibly in the same grade, as the respondent practitioner.

The doctor is entitled to receive notice of the setting up of the panel, and its terms of reference, and to be given not less than twenty-one days in which to prepare his case. He should be provided with copies of correspondence and, at his request, a list of witnesses with a note of the main points on which they can give evidence, unless the Chairman of the panel decides otherwise. The practitioner may appear personally, or be represented, legally or otherwise. The panel makes its report in two parts. The first part sets out the findings of fact and the second records the panel's opinion as to whether the practitioner was at fault and may recommend certain disciplinary action. The doctor receives a copy of the first part of the report and may, within a period of fourteen days, submit proposals for correction of facts which the panel may accept or reject.

The report is then passed to the employing authority, and before they meet to decide what action to take, the doctor is informed of the substance of the second part of the panel's report and is given the opportunity of making a plea in mitigation before the final decision is taken.

The above has set out what should happen and what doubtless would happen if all concerned understood the regulations, appreciated the need for each step, and had nothing else to do. But what actually occurs in this hard practical world in which we live? Leaving aside the senior grades which have special rights of appeal to the Secretary of State if they consider that their appointments are being unfairly terminated, the overriding fact is that once things have got to the point of disciplinary action, there is often no future for the doctor in the hospital concerned, quite irrespective of the merits of the case. Few such cases occur, but when they do it is not uncommon to find that the hospital administrator has, off his own bat or with the agreement or encouragement of a consultant, dismissed the doctor, possibly after a travesty of a quasi-judicial enquiry. The doctor leaves the hospital and it may be some time later that he thinks to take advice on the matter. It can seldom be to his interest to insist on the full formal procedure which would entail his attending before the panel at, perhaps, considerable personal inconvenience and expense. Often his protection society will be able to hammer out some agreement whereby the dismissal is withdrawn and the doctor or the authority give retrospective notice with appropriate payment.

One such case merits special mention. The doctor, in his first pre-registration post, was suspected of being an imposter. The hospital management committee convened a panel to consider his dismissal, three eminent consultants being appointed, all of whom held posts at the same hospital as the houseman and, therefore, could hardly be thought to approach their task with open minds. The houseman was only told of the meeting three days before, was not told of the charge against him, was not given time to take advice, was not permitted to be heard in his own defence, or even to be present or represented at the meeting. His instructions were simply that he should hold himself in readiness to be summoned if required, but in the event the panel found no need for his presence. So utterly ignorant of the requirements of the regulations and of the rules of natural justice were these eminent gentlemen that they solemnly met and duly recommended the houseman's dismissal in circumstances such as these. There was nothing malicious about their action—they simply did not know any better and never thought to query their own authority or procedure. When the houseman reported these strange happenings, it was thought prudent to take opinions from two registrars in the hospital—registrars being very well placed to know precisely what goes on in both the higher and lower echelons of hospital life. The reasons for the hospital authority's anxieties were quickly apparent; one does not expect that a houseman, even one in his first post, would, having scrubbed up in the theatre, remove his cap and scratch the back of his head with his gloved hand. This and other irregularities made it apparent that, were the correct procedures to be invoked, the result must be the same. The houseman's interests were therefore best met by an agreement that the dismissal be cancelled, the record expunged, and he be permitted to give one month's notice, for which period payment would be made but he would not be required to work.

This chapter has dealt largely with the dry bones of law and regulations. But before one gets to the bones there are matters of flesh and blood, soma and psyche, to be considered, and where they receive adequate consideration, it will seldom be necessary to trouble the law. Here faults occur on both sides. Some newly qualified practitioners tend to look on those without medical degrees as belonging to lower strata of evolution, and their approach to the administrative staff reflects this viewpoint. There can be little doubt that a really first-class senior hospital administrator contributes much to the welfare of the patients, and the resident who is prepared to acknowledge the standing and experience of such administrators will, in all probability, find that the mutual respect engendered will smooth his path through the hospital.

On the other hand, by no means all hospital administrators are first- or even second-class and sometimes rank injustice occurs. A houseman in the North Country sought permission to leave his post without giving the full month's notice as he had been offered a post which was approved for the higher degree he wished to take, the offer being conditional upon his taking up the appointment by a certain date. The consultant in charge of the department supported his application and this was agreed by the hospital authority, but they later sought to make him pay a sum equal to what his gross earnings would have been had he worked out the full month's notice. Such a claim was entirely without legal sanction. In the first place, the authority had agreed to the termination of the contract and, in the second, even had the doctor acted in breach of his contract the authority's claim would have been limited to such sum as they could prove they had lost by the breach, and the claim was made before the houseman had so much as left his post. The administrator was informed by the houseman's protection society that the member had been advised that he was in no way indebted to the authority, and after some correspondence the account was cancelled, though not with very good grace.

Since the 1975 Employment Protection Act, NHS Disciplinary Procedures have been adopted by some employing authorities, incorporating the main provision of the Code of Practice issued by the Advisory, Conciliation and Arbitration Service. The wider promulgation of Disciplinary Procedures has led to an increase in usage, often in circumstances where a tactful discussion and friendly counselling would probably be of greater benefit to all concerned.

The procedures provide for written notification of allegations, opportunity of representation at any hearing, and a right of appeal. There is a tendency to call an informal meeting initially, ostensibly to decide whether a disciplinary hearing is appropriate, but experience has shown that too often the informality is used to help the administration frame the charges. Practitioners finding themselves in a situation which may involve Disciplinary Procedures should contact the POWAR or IRO of the BMA before making any statement or replying to questions. The protection societies can assist also if required, but local help is often better able to resolve such matters quickly.

The roles for protection societies on the one hand and the BMA on the other can be confusing. Legal actions, GMC complaints, and disciplinary enquiries under the Terms and Conditions of Service are primarily for protection societies. Grievances, Whitley Council appeals and ACAS procedures are primarily for the BMA. I am indebted to the BMA's Chief Industrial Officer for the following paragraphs on the BMA as a trade union.

> Since its formation in 1832 the BMA has continually sought to promote the corporate interests of its members. So it can be properly described as having undertaken the functions of a trade union, though the Association has had other functions besides these, notably those of a professional and scientific body. The BMA has continued ever since to negotiate collectively with those bodies which have funded medical care, whether publicly or privately sponsored—that is, the State or the insurance agencies. Indeed such union functions started as far back as the 1830s, when the Provincial Medical and Surgical Association (as the BMA was then called) acted to raise the remuneration and standing of poor law medical officers. Furthermore, these functions have been undertaken on behalf of both those doctors whose status is that of an independent contractor—for example, general practitioners—and those who are employees—for example, in the hospital service and other disciplines.
>
> If the BMA has always undertaken union-type functions it may well be asked why so much significance is now being attached to the development of this side of the Association's activities. Several factors have recently emerged and combined to give a new perspective and prominence to the trade union role. These same factors have also made it more difficult (if not impossible) to sustain the traditional view of the BMA's activities as being wholly and simply professional.
>
> While the BMA was able to persuade others (and the profession) that its active defence of members' corporate interests was no

more than an extension of its professional functions, there was no pressing need to adopt the legal status of a trade union. Until 1975 the BMA retained a restrictive clause in its Articles which specifically prevented the Association from pursuing trade union objectives. Whenever the BMA found itself in dispute with Government over the pay and conditions of service of members, any possible constitutional and legal difficulties were avoided by adopting the guise of the British Medical Guild, which was established in 1949 for the purpose of taking union-type action which would have been prohibited by the Articles. The guild was a phantom body formed for the purpose of raising and administering funds (drawn from the defence funds of the craft committees) to support a threat of withdrawal from the NHS. As recently as 1975 after the resignation of the Kindersley Review Body, the BMA used this technique to avoid its status as a limited liability company being put at risk by trade union action. In 1975 the Association collected the resignations of general practitioners against the possibility of the Secretary of State taking similar action.

Industrial Relations Legislation

This advantageous arrangement was able to continue unhindered until 1971 when the Industrial Relations Act was implemented. However, in order to strengthen the legal control over trade union affairs, this Act made it unlawful for any organisation to act as a trade union unless it was properly registered as such. The BMA persuaded the Government to set up a special register to deal with the difficulties which it and other professional bodies would have experienced in registering as trade unions. But this Act had so fundamentally altered industrial relations law, by seeking to codify in legal terms the status of trade unions and their actions, that it removed for ever any possibility of reverting to the convenient and relatively uncomplicated arrangements formerly available to the BMA.

In 1974 the Industrial Relations Act was repealed and replaced by the Trade Union and Labour Relations Act. The special register for professional organisations was abolished, and the BMA was by definition a trade union. The BMA was obliged to register as an independent trade union if it were to be protected by law in any action it might take as a trade union, and also to obtain certain benefits accorded to trade unions under recent legislation.

Alongside these legal developments other factors have added impetus to the expansion of the BMA's trade union role. The acquisition of this new status had a catalytic effect by initiating a reappraisal of the Association's structure and services to the member. Once the psychological hurdle of the BMA registering as a union had been overcome there seemed to be no reason why the Association should not take full advantage of the benefits now available to it. Hence the introduction of the Place of Work Accredited Representative (POWAR) scheme and the positive decision that representatives should participate in the range of industrial relations machinery being established in the NHS.

3 The Police

Information to Police

Like all nicely brought up boys and girls, the medical student or practitioner of today has a fundamental basic concept that the policeman is a trusty friend from whom no harm or ill could possibly originate. This belief, instilled and nurtured at a very early age, survives completely unscathed through rag weeks, Easter rugger tours, and hospital cup finals. So it is that the newly fledged practitioner, far from feeling any need for caution when faced with the man in blue, tends rather to become expansive and to welcome an ally who may, he feels, be able to assist in the disposal of a somewhat difficult patient or otherwise help with his greater experience of the current medico-legal problem.

The policeman, on his part, whether or not well versed in the power and force of infantile indoctrination, knows well the strength of his position. He knows that members of what he perhaps regards as the non-criminal classes have a tendency to tell him the truth and the whole truth upon request. He may indeed have some reservations on his part in respect of rag weeks, Easter rugger tours, and hospital cup finals, but by and large he regards the junior hospital doctor as a helpful collaborator or, at times, a far from powerful adversary.

The scene, then, is the casualty department, the time Saturday evening shortly after the pubs have closed when, in answer to his cue—a phone call from the casualty sister—the provisionally registered house physician, standing in for the casualty officer, enters to find the stage occupied by one large policeman and one noisy, incoherent, bloodstained character smelling like a brewery. Not without some difficulty, the examination is completed and the doctor emerges from the cubicle to find the guardian of the law with pencil poised. 'Well, what's the matter with our friend, do you think?' 'Oh, he's had a skinful right enough. I can't find much else the matter but we'll keep him here overnight just to be sure.'

So far so good; but before he gives any further information regarding anything which passed between his patient and himself, or anything which he found on examination, the doctor should reflect that in general the police are in exactly the same position as any other third party. They have no right to come between patient and doctor, and if they want a report from the doctor then the patient's consent is necessary, and it is for the police—not the doctor—to obtain that consent.

It is reasonable to tell the policeman who has brought a patient in that it is or is not proposed to admit him. If, in a case of serious injury, it is intended to ask the police to contact relatives, then it is reasonable to give such information as it is thought should be immediately conveyed to the relatives, but this is all. Professional secrecy, which, one must always bear in mind, exists for the benefit of the patient, not as an excuse for the doctor, precludes one going further.

There are a number of exceptions to this general ethical principle and the most common one concerns the drunken driver. The Road Traffic Act 1972 lays it down that, following an accident, a constable in uniform may require any person whom he has reasonable cause to believe was driving or attempting to drive the vehicle to take a breath test when at a hospital as a patient. It is required that the doctor in charge be first informed of the intention, and he is entitled to object on the ground that the provision of the specimen or the requirement to provide it would be prejudicial to the proper care or treatment of the patient. Should the breath test indicate that the patient has a blood alcohol exceeding the prescribed limit, the patient can be required to provide a specimen of blood or urine, but again, the doctor must first be notified and he is entitled to object should he feel that the provision of a specimen, the requirement to provide it, or the necessary warning that failure to provide a specimen may make the patient liable to imprisonment, fine, and disqualification, would be prejudicial to his proper care or treatment. It is not part of the hospital doctor's duty to take any specimen required under this Act nor to provide any equipment, though he might arrange that the patient be given reasonable privacy.

The question of consent for such investigation is nothing whatever to do with the doctor, being a matter entirely between constable and patient. As consent is necessary it follows that no specimen can be taken from the unconscious patient for police purposes, nor from one who is too drunk to understand what is being required of him. As to the patient's ability to understand, it would seem from the case of R. *v* Nicholls* that where the constable reasonably and honestly believes that the patient can hear and understand, then the patient can be convicted.

A second occasion where the police have a right to information is where they are seeking to identify the vehicle driver or cycle rider alleged to have committed an offence under the Road Traffic Act. Section 168 of the 1972 Act requires any person so requested to give the police such information as he has which may lead to the identification.

It was in 1973 that following a road accident the driver and passenger of a car involved departed from the scene in haste without leaving any name or address. That evening a man and a girl attended a doctor's surgery saying that they had been involved in an accident and seeking treatment. The doctor provided the necessary treatment and at the same time he advised that the police be contacted. Subsequently the police approached the doctor and asked for the names and addresses of these patients. The doctor objected on the grounds of professional confidence but was later convicted under Section 168 and the conviction was upheld on appeal to the divisional Court†.

There are then the cases where a doctor may reasonably feel that his public duty as a citizen must take precedence over the normal requirement of professional secrecy. At the time of one celebrated murder hunt, no fewer than five doctors contacted the author to say that they had patients who had confessed to having committed the murder and what should they do about it. Where murder or other very serious crime is in question, perhaps all are agreed that public duty must take pride of place. The doctor reporting the patient's statement to the police does so appreciating that the patient might subsequently sue him for breach of the implied contract of professional secrecy. This risk he must take. It is a very small one, and his protection society will certainly give him their full support.

When we come to crimes of somewhat lesser degree, however, there is ample scope for a considerable divergence of opinion. The doctor must act according to the dictates of his conscience and, provided he does so, he has little to fear. Should any legal complica-

* (1972) 1 WLR 502; (1972) All ER 186.

† Hunter *v* Mann (1974) QB 767. *Medical Defence Union Annual Report* 1974, page 18.

tions ensue, he may rest assured that his protection society will not seek to judge him nor to substitute their conscience for his.

Regarding petty crimes, there is more general agreement of opinion. It is no part of a doctor's job to act as a common informer regarding matters which come to his notice in the course of his professional duties. Occasionally, the police circularise doctors regarding people they wish to interview, and such circulars usually state the nature of the crime involved and the type of illness or injury from which the wanted man is believed to suffer. There is no compulsion on the doctor to respond to such circulars; they are requests, not orders, and the doctor's action or inaction must depend largely on the nature of the crime. In general he will, it is thought, feel it proper to comply, but there are exceptions. Doctors in a large northern city were circularised to the effect that the body of a new born female child had been found in suspicious circumstances. They were asked to supply a list of all their patients known to be pregnant. Such a request was considered unreasonable and largely useless, and the advice of the Medical Protection Society was that such lists should not be provided. One doctor, however, who had an unmarried patient who was overdue and had disappeared from her lodgings was advised to give the police full information about her.

Another problem regarding reports to the police arises when the doctor is faced with a pregnant girl who must have been below the age of consent when conception occurred. A crime has been committed and a doctor who fails to disclose such information may fear that his inaction could lead to a charge being brought against him. However, in Sykes *v* Director of Public Prosecutions*, Lord Denning said,

> 'Non-disclosure may sometimes be justified or excused on the ground of privilege. For instance, if a lawyer has been told by his client that he has committed a felony, it would be no misprision in the lawyer not to report it to the police, for he might in good faith claim that he was under a duty to keep it confidential. Likewise with doctor and patient, and clergyman and parishioner.'

The Criminal Law Act 1967 effected the disappearance of the offence of misprision of felony, and the doctor is in no danger from

* H. of L., June 1961.

maintaining silence provided that he does not accept, or agree to accept, any consideration for so doing.

Apart from the legal aspects, however, what action should the doctor take? If, as is most probable, the girl's parents are aware of her condition, then the doctor can reasonably leave it to them to decide whether or not the matter should be reported. Should the parents not be so aware, the girl should be strongly urged to break the news to them; but of course she may refuse. It is seldom that an experienced doctor cannot persuade such a patient to confide in her mother. A powerful argument is to point out that mothers were not born yesterday, that the information is bound to come out sooner or later, and that it is one's usual experience that the mother is more upset by her daughter's failure to tell her of her trouble than by the fact of the pregnancy itself. Should persuasion fail, however, the doctor's duty is as always to his patient, and he must do what he considers to be in the patient's best interest, and professional secrecy, which, as has been said, exists for the benefit of the patient, must not be allowed to operate against it. In dealing with a girl of such tender years, it is probable that the doctor will decide that he must inform the parents, but perhaps he will find that the threat of his intention to do so will be sufficient to cause his patient to act and thus save him the necessity of so doing.

Epileptic Drivers

It is perhaps convenient to consider here the question of the epileptic driver. The Vehicles and Motor Driving Licenses Act 1969 improved on a grossly unsatisfactory situation by permitting epileptics in certain categories to obtain driving licences, and this Act was later consolidated into the Road Traffic Act 1972. The present position is determined by the terms of the 1972 Act and regulations made under it.

Whilst epilepsy remains a relevant disability, which type of disability in general prohibits the issue of a licence, there are exceptions. An epileptic may be granted a driving licence if he has been free from any epileptic attacks for at least two years. Where an applicant has had such attacks only whilst asleep for the past three years, a licence may be granted provided that he has a history of attacks only whilst asleep extending over more than the three year period. The licensing authority in either case requires also to be satisfied that the applicant's driving would not be likely to be a source of danger to the public.

A holder of a driving licence is required to inform the licensing authority should he have any disability which affects or is likely to affect his fitness to drive, unless he does not expect the disability to last for more than three months. Where the doctor may come into the picture is where the Licensing Centre becomes aware of a patient's disability and asks him to consent to his doctor supplying information. Should the patient refuse or should the information supplied by the doctor to the medical adviser at the Licensing Centre leave the latter in doubt, then the patient may be required to undergo a medical examination.

But where stands the doctor who becomes aware that his epileptic patient, whose fits do not bring him within the exempted categories, is in fact driving? First let it be said that epilepsy in this context is no different from any other condition which affects a patient's ability to drive safely, and the doctor's problem is then precisely the same in all such cases.

The legal duty to inform the Licensing Centre is on the patient. Before, however, he can be expected to perform this duty he must know that he suffers from such a disability and this point should be borne in mind when considering what a patient should be told. Indeed there are many cases in which the patient, although told the nature of his disability, might not realise its effect on his ability to drive unless his doctor gives him clear advice on this point. Should the patient ignore such advice, the doctor, it is suggested, should write to him, retaining as always a copy of the letter, pointing out the dangers to the public and to the patient himself, and urging that the Licensing Centre be informed.

This is perhaps as far as the doctor should go with the vast majority of patients. Exceptionally he may feel that the danger to the public is such that he should confer with the medical adviser at the Licensing Centre, and he may think it proper first to advise his patient of his intention to do so. In the case of a public service driver however, it might in certain circumstances be considered necessary to inform the patient that if he does not voluntarily seek alternative employment, it is the doctor's intention to communicate with his employer.

Harm to Children

There has been much publicity of late concerning the battered baby syndrome, and the suspicion that a child's injuries result not from accident but from deliberate acts of the parents immediately poses the question as to whether the police or other authority should be informed. In the grosser cases there is no doubt; the doctor's duty is to his patient, the child, and the child's interests demand that the police, the community health physician or the NSPCC should be informed forthwith. Should the parents later endeavour to bring an action against the doctor, his protection society will indeed be happy to support him. The lesser cases are more difficult. To report such cases will likely result in the child being removed from the parent's care, and this may or may not be in the child's best interests. One such case concerned a woman who had marked hysteric traits but, nevertheless, had always appeared to be a very adequate mother. She attended her GP's surgery with lesions on both legs, the size and shape of a penny. These proved markedly resistant to treatment and were never seen to be less than fully developed, so that it was not long before they were confidently diagnosed as artifacts produced, no doubt, by applying hot pennies to the skin. One day however, to the GP's dismay, the patient arrived with her four-year-old daughter who also showed a precisely similar lesion, and the problem was how the child's future welfare could be secured without having her removed from what had always been thought to be a good home. The GP prescribed treatment and asked that the girl be brought back the following day, meanwhile arranging that his friend, a consultant dermatologist, should just happen to arrive at the surgery at the appropriate time. On receiving a nod of agreement from his colleague, the GP then proceeded to tell the mother in no uncertain terms precisely what would happen to her if she ever produced any further harm to her child. The child's lesion healed rapidly, no further lesions appeared, but, such is the ambivalence of the hysteric, the mother continued to produce similar lesions on her own legs and to attend regularly for their treatment.

Enquiries Regarding Oneself

It has been said earlier in this chapter that there are occasions when one should give all possible information to the police. There are also circumstances under which the less said, the better. The contrast between what occurred in the following two cases will point the moral.

A house surgeon telephoned the author one morning to say that the police were on their way to interview him about a complaint made by a seventeen-year-old girl whom he had seen in the casualty department the previous day, the accusation being that he had fondled her breasts. On being asked his side of the story, he stated that the patient was complaining of a painful eye and he diagnosed conjunctivitis which he felt might be phlyctenular. Thinking that phlyctenular conjunctivitis could be tuberculous, and the TB could interfere with the menstrual cycle, he asked about her periods and, finding that she was some days overdue, he felt her breasts to see if they were engorged. It was explained to the house surgeon that, if this matter ever went into court, it would largely hinge upon whether any expert could be found who would support his line of reasoning and examination, and he was told that it was not thought likely that such an expert could be found. As he wished firmly to deny any improper motive in his examination, he was advised that, to the first question the police asked, he should say 'nothing but a normal examination took place', and to each and all further questions he should reply 'I have nothing to add'. The house surgeon carried out the advice given and nothing was heard for a few days, when the hospital administrator came on the telephone. It appeared that the police had returned and persuaded him that all they required was a short statement from the doctor so that they could assure the girl's parents that all was well. It was pointed out that just as a doctor cannot prescribe treatment until he has examined the patient, so the police cannot say what they will do with information until they know what that information may be. Nothing further was heard of this matter.

The opposite side of the coin is illustrated by what occurred when a teenage girl consulted her dentist, complaining of pain in the lower jaw. The dentist had found enlarged cervical glands and proposed to X-ray the jaw. Finding that he was out of film he sent his chairside assistant to collect some from the storeroom downstairs. While she was away, the dentist put his hand inside the girl's dress to feel for enlarged axillary glands. No complaint was made, the X-ray was taken, some treatment carried out and a letter given addressed to a hospital consultant. The next thing the dentist knew was that he was asked to go down to the police station as a complaint had been made to the effect that he had touched the patient's breasts. It is a tribute to the charm of the police, if not to the common sense of the dentist, that he spent no less than two and a half hours in the police station explaining precisely what had happened, while notes were taken of all he said. He was then told that he might be charged. Later the Summons was served upon him and it then occurred to him to contact the Medical Protection Society. On interview it quickly became apparent that the crucial question would be whether, in the opinion of such experts as might attend the court, dentists should pursue glands below the clavicle. An immediate telephone call to the senior consultant dental surgeon in the part of the country concerned proved most helpful as he fully supported the dentist's action, and on contacting the second senior consultant his view was that while he would not, perhaps, have acted in this way, he would certainly support a dentist's right to do so. It was the second consultant who telephoned the following day to say that he had been approached by the police with a request that he consider giving expert evidence in a case of alleged indecent assault against a dentist. He had replied that he might very likely be appearing for the defence, adding that his senior colleague would be with him. Nothing further occurred for a few days when, by a stroke of good fortune, a junior consultant in the district wrote seeking advice about a proposed report to the police which he was in the process of preparing. While in no way attempting to alter his views, to which of course he was fully entitled, it was thought not improper to inform him that the case would be defended all the way and that he would find two senior consultants appearing as experts for the defence. In the event the charge was dropped. Although, then, all was well in the end, the dentist suffered weeks of acute anxiety brought on not by the patient's complaint—the police will seldom act in such cases where it is one person's word against another—but by his own naivety.

4 Solicitors

The relationships between the local medical and legal professions vary widely from one area to another. In some, and particularly where a medico-legal society or some liaison between medical and legal societies exists, they may be of the most cordial nature. In others, the doctors may be suspicious of the lawyers, and the lawyers may feel that there is little hope of obtaining reliable medical opinion and a willing medical witness locally. In the majority there is, perhaps, a degree of failure by each side to appreciate the problems, duties, and attitudes of the other, and from such failure suspicion and distrust are bred.

Reports

Perhaps the first solicitor's letter a newly qualified doctor will receive will be one seeking a report in respect of a patient he has treated, perhaps in the casualty department where no senior person has been involved. A recent occurrence in a teaching hospital illustrates most of the things which can go wrong following such a simple request. The first letter from the solicitors was addressed to 'The Registrar', who, it would seem, is thought by many solicitors to be some form of administrative official, and, it being apparently nobody's job to open such vaguely addressed letters, it lay unclaimed for some weeks. A second letter followed, this time addressed to the Secretary/Superintendent, which was referred by the administrator to a registrar of the consultant under whose care the patient had been. The letter stated that the solicitors were acting for the patient and asked for a report on his original injuries, present condition, and prognosis, and concluded by saying that the solicitors would be responsible for the doctor's fee for the report. It was in all respects a perfectly proper letter. The registrar replied stating that a report had been prepared and would be forwarded when, and not before, he received the patient's written consent plus his fee. The solicitors, not unnaturally, were exceedingly irritated, forwarded the fee, refused to supply their client's written consent, stating that their word that they were acting for the patient was sufficient, and said a few very unpleasant things about the attitude of the registrar. In such circumstances, if events had required further contact between doctor and lawyer—if perhaps the case had gone into Court—the patient's interests might well have been prejudiced by the ill-feeling engendered.

What went wrong? After the initial error by the solicitors in addressing the first letter, the next difficulty arose because of the rules of the particular hospital which stated that reports should not be sent to any third party before the written consent of the patient had been obtained and also recommended that payment in advance be requested. It is, of course, essential that reports on a patient are not provided without valid consent, but a report to a patient's solicitor is essentially the same as a report to the patient himself, and where a solicitor states that he is acting for the patient no further consent is required. Regarding the question of fees, where a solicitor says he will be responsible for a doctor's fees, it is surely discourteous, to say the least, to demand payment in advance—how would a doctor feel if on seeking a solicitor's advice he was met with sealed lips and an outstretched palm? Where no statement is made regarding fees in the solicitor's letter it is certainly reasonable, and indeed advisable, to enquire on this point before providing the report, but when the initial letter gives the necessary assurance, an account for a reasonable amount can be submitted with confidence. The operative word is of course 'reasonable'.

A casualty officer submitted, at the request of a solicitor, a report regarding a small simple injury which an ex-patient had suffered. The report ran to only three or four lines and its compilation could not have taken more than a few minutes of the casualty officer's time. He submitted a wholly disproportionate account and was most aggrieved to receive in due course a cheque for half the amount claimed. After some acrimonious correspondence on the subject he sought advice as to what steps he could take to enforce payment. He was advised, however, to bank the cheque and take no further action. This unwelcome advice was based on the fact that the solicitors had carried out their promise to be responsible for the doctor's reasonable fees. Had an attempt been made to enforce payment through the County Court the solicitors would have been able to put up a successful defence, as it was inconceivable that the Court could have valued the report at more than the sum offered. The result might have been that the doctor would have become liable to pay the costs of the defence.

When considering how much to charge, the first point is whether a fee can be charged at all. Doctors employed in a National Health Service hospital are not entitled to charge for reports made to a patient or, with his consent, to an interested third party when the patient is still under observation or treatment in the hospital at the time the report is requested, unless it is necessary to carry out a special examination for the purpose of the report. Provided then that a fee can properly be charged the amount is dependent upon the time involved, the complexity of the case, whether a simple statement of fact or an opinion which necessitates due consideration is required, and the status of the doctor concerned. Fees might vary from £5 to £50, although it is seldom that a houseman or registrar could justify a fee exceeding £20.

Having made the report, difficulties are not necessarily at an end, for weeks, and sometimes months, will pass without payment being received and letters to the solicitors may go unanswered. The doctor has, indeed, little to worry about. His fee will almost certainly arrive in due course and the usual reason for delay is that the case with which the report is concerned is a legally aided one and the solicitor is not in funds until the case is concluded and costs are duly taxed. Granted that this delay is not the fault of the solicitor, it is none the less somewhat galling for the doctor whose hospital appointment is approaching its end and who finds himself unable to obtain either his fee or indeed, not infrequently, to obtain any response to his enquiries. While the doctor should not be importunate, the solicitor who is not prepared to accept personal responsibility for the doctor's fees, as recommended by the Law Society, might at least be expected to explain that delay must be anticipated.

To redress the balance of anything written so far, which might give the impression that doctors tend to be unreasonable regarding fees when dealing with solicitors, the experiences of a general practitioner some years ago might be quoted. This doctor had occasion to require his solicitor to proceed abroad regarding some property he had acquired. While discussing the project in the solicitor's office one day, the solicitor mentioned that he would have to be vaccinated and the practitioner suggested that he call in on his way home from his office and he would be pleased to see to that matter for him. The solicitor duly called in, was vaccinated and stayed for a drink or two. He proceeded abroad, the business was transacted and, as expected, a very lengthy and substantial account was rendered. What was not expected, however, was one item on the account which read 'To visiting your surgery to be vaccinated, two guineas'. When told of this matter the writer suggested that the riposte was, when settling the account, to enclose a bill for five guineas for the vaccination, deduct this amount from the total and then change solicitors. On recounting this happening to a solicitor, the reply was that this almost equalled the classic story of the solicitor's bill which included the items 'To seeing you in the street and crossing over to talk to you, one guinea' and 'To crossing back on finding it wasn't you, one guinea'.

Witnesses and Their Fees

The Council of the Law Society has expressed the view that when a solicitor engages the services of a professional witness, he should assume personal liability for the payment of the proper fee of that witness unless at the time the services are requested the solicitor makes it quite clear to the witness concerned that he would not be personally responsible for the payment of the fees involved, and that the witness must look to the lay client for payment. Therefore, it is perfectly proper for a doctor to ascertain the position regarding his fees at the outset, and to do so may well avoid misunderstanding and possible ill-feeling later. There are two types of witness, witnesses of fact and expert witnesses. The essential difference between these is not—as some consultants appear to imagine—a question of one's status in the hospital hierarchy, but simply whether the witness is required to give evidence on matters on which he has first hand knowledge, or whether he is called, because of his particular experience and qualifications in the matter before the Court, to draw deductions from the facts disclosed, and to advise as to their implications. While, then, a houseman is unlikely in the extreme to appear as an expert witness, there is no reason whatever why a consultant on the topmost rung of the ladder should not be a witness of fact.

A particular difficulty arises in matrimonial cases where both husband and wife are the doctor's patients and he is asked for a report and to attend Court. He must, of course, inform the husband's solicitors of facts learned only in his attendance upon the husband and vice versa, but it is suggested that he should inform each solicitor that both parties are his patients and ask that, if required to give evidence in Court, he be subpoenaed. This will make it clear that he is attending Court because he is compelled to do so, and in giving his evidence—which matter is referred to in the chapter on Court Procedure—he should make it clear that he is there to assist the Court to come to a just decision and not to promote the interests of one patient against another.

Regarding criminal cases, a doctor called to give evidence of fact on behalf of the Crown or of the defence may receive a professional witness allowance which at the time of writing is as follows:

Attendance in excess of four hours or lesser time, with locum	£41.60
Attendance of four hours or less, without locum together with travel allowance	£20.80

A whole-time medical officer in the National Health Service is not precluded from receiving a professional witness allowance, but in assessing this, the Court may have regard to the circumstances of his employment.

In the High Court, a doctor appearing as a witness of fact may hope to receive a fee of £50 to £75 per day. In the County Court, a fee of £40 to £50 a day may be expected. Travelling and subsistence allowance may also be allowed, as may expenses incurred should a locum have to be paid. It is essential that in discussing fees the doctor assures himself that the agreed fee will be paid for each day's attendance at Court whether or not he is called upon to give evidence. In coming to the agreement, the doctor on his side must be reasonable and appreciate that it is often impossible for the solicitor to judge precisely when the doctor will be required, and that he delays and uncertainties are not the fault of the solicitor but of the system, which appears often to work on the principle that whoever else's time is wasted, that of the Court must never be.

While the attendance of a witness of fact may be enforced by means of a subpoena—together with, in civil cases, conduct money to ensure that the witness has the means of travelling to the Court—no one can be compelled to appear as an expert witness, and a doctor on being approached should agree his fee before accepting such an invitation. An expert witness is entitled to recover the full amount of his fees as agreed with the solicitor calling on him, notwithstanding that the full amount might not be allowed on taxation of costs. The fees for such expert advice which a successful litigant may recover as part of his costs on taxation are at the discretion of the Court and generally fall within the following range:

1 High Court—£100 to £150 a day, plus £25 to £50 for qualifying
2 County Court—about £40 a day, plus £20 for qualifying
3 Criminal Courts—such amount as the Court may consider reasonable

The legal term 'qualifying' refers to the preparatory work which expert witnesses undertake before giving evidence. It includes study of the case notes and pleadings together with references to recognised textbooks and relevant professional literature.

Hospital Notes and X-rays

In an NHS hospital the notes and X-rays are the property of the hospital authority, and it is for the authority and not for the doctor—although the consultant in charge of the case will normally be consulted—to determine whether they should be made available to the patient's solicitors or other third party. Each case must be judged on its merits and it is pertinent to consider the purpose for which the notes may be required. In some cases of industrial or road accident where an insurance claim arises, it may be quite reasonable to make the notes available so that the solicitors have a clear view of the degree of injury suffered by their client, and under these circumstances the solicitors will probably be quite prepared to confirm that they are not considering any legal proceedings against the hospital or member of the medical staff. In other cases, there will be obvious *prima facie* grounds for action against the hospital. Where some obvious error, e.g. amputation of the wrong finger, has occurred there is clearly a case in negligence; the patient's solicitors could, without difficulty, obtain a Court Order for the discovery of the documents and, again, the hospital authority will in all probability agree to release them.

Third, there occur requests for notes and X-rays for no apparent reason, or perhaps a vague comment regarding complaints in respect of the treatment given. In such cases, a request for a copy of the notes will probably be refused. No one wishes to be unfair to the patient or to hide from him clear evidence of negligence, but there is a world of difference between hiding essential evidence and facilitating a patient's solicitor going on a fishing expedition through the notes to see if there is anything on to which he can hang any or all of the patient's complaints. A doctor is not an insurer that no harm will befall his patient, and a fact that a complication has occurred does not of itself justify hunting through the notes for points to criticise.

The Administration of Justice Act 1970* introduced two procedures by which in personal injury cases the Court could order disclosure of documents. Section 31 permits a person likely to be a party to legal proceedings arising from personal injuries or death to apply for disclosure of documents relevant to the action. The application may be opposed, but if successful the hospital authority or doctor will be required to disclose relevant records.

Section 32 relates to proceedings already in being and permits a party to the action to apply to the High Court for disclosure of records held by a person not a party to the action.

For some years after the coming into operation of this Act, it was customary, and in accordance with judgments of the Court of Appeal, for the disclosure of medical records to be made to the medical adviser of the applicant. In 1978, however, the House of Lords ruled, in the case of McIvor *v* the Southern Health and Social Securities Board (Northern Ireland)† that disclosure should be to the applicant himself. The effect of this ruling is that a patient may obtain access to his own medical records, and to the records of other patients should the Court consider such records relevant to the action.

Since the McIvor decision it has become commonplace for solicitors to demand production of records, claiming that the House of Lords decision gave them such a right. When this occurs it is pointed out that no such right exists, as McIvor determines only to whom such disclosure as the Court might order should be made. The solicitor may then be invited to submit a draft affidavit, that is the document he would produce to the Court in support of his application for disclosure, and consideration of this allows one to decide whether disclosure should be made without more ado, or whether application to the Court should be opposed.

Private patients and their solicitors sometimes take the view that the X-ray plates belong to the patient, and, on occasion, attempt to withhold the radiologist's fees until they are produced. This view has always been successfully opposed by the Medical Protection Society, which holds that what the patient has paid for is the radiologist's opinion and the films are but the raw material from which that opinion is derived. Unless, then, it has been previously arranged that

* Relevant sections now replaced by Sections 33 and 34 of the Supreme Court Act 1981.

† (1978) 1 WLR 757.

the patient will have the films, it is not considered that the radiologist is required to part with them.

The very fact that notes may at some later date be made available to the patient's solicitors should lead to a certain caution in their compilation, for notes are intended to give information about the patient, and if they, unfortunately, give information about the doctor as well, he may well find himself in an indefensible position. Consider this casualty card:

'23.55 another M/c accident!
Dazed and grazed—NBI.'

But it wasn't 'NBI' as later events proved, so how could it be said that the casualty officer had carried out a careful methodical examination against evidence like that? Another casualty officer used the phrase 'bruised and boozed', but the patient turned out to be more than bruised and such an entry would hardly have done the casualty officer's reputation any good in Court.

Neither humour nor evidence of irritation have any place in hospital notes, nor have personal abbreviations. To endeavour to understand what successive housemen have implied when they have written up the patient's notes in the same manner as they were accustomed to taking lecture notes often proves impossible. Apart from the irritation this causes it may result in misfortune, if not more, for the patient, and a subsequent negligence action against the doctor. A senior registrar referred a boy to a surgical registrar in the minor operations theatre. The notes read:

'L I G T now
R I G T N 12/12 ago—satisfactory
Minor ops
For wedge excision under GA'

It was certainly not prudent for the surgical registrar to operate at all on such instructions, but suffice it to say that the protection organisation to which the senior registrar belonged shared in the settlement which in due course had to be negotiated in respect of an operation having been carried out on the wrong foot. It would have been better for both patient and doctor had the latter written underneath 'W T H D Y M' and sent the patient back.

There is another peculiarity which carries its own dangers, and that is what the writer has come to refer to as 'teaching hospital notes'. This may be quite unfair and, indeed, it may merely be that when, in a teaching hospital, notes of this type are written then they are more likely to come to the attention of a protection society at a later date. Their characteristic is that on the day of admission reams are written—page after page is filled with negative findings; the dresser, the junior houseman, the senior houseman, the registrar, the senior registrar and even the consultant may join in. The signs found do not, of course, always agree. The big toe may appear to have been going both up and down if not sideways. Two years later, of course, it is quite impossible to determine who wrote what. Was this the view of one who is now a transatlantic associate professor, or the mere outpourings of a dresser who first appeared on the ward the previous week and who felt that anything was better than a blank page, and do students' opinions really merit mention in the patient's folder? After the first fine flurry, however, one searches in vain for a clear chronological picture of how things developed. Perhaps everyone got writer's cramp, or it may have been that no one had the time to find the place to make further entries. At this point one turns with relief to the nursing report which often proves of great assistance.

The Solicitor as Antagonist

While this chapter has been written with the hope of promoting a better understanding between doctor and lawyer, there may come a time when a doctor finds himself being attacked. The solicitor who rings up, does not state his business but would 'just happen to be in the doctor's neighbourhood that afternoon and would like to see him for ten minutes', should be viewed with considerable suspicion, as should the gentleman on the phone who 'just wishes to confirm that Mrs Snooks attended the ante-natal clinic yesterday'. No statement, verbal or written, should be given until the solicitor has stated in writing for whom he is acting.

Where hospitals or doctors fail to observe the traditional and ethical courtesies, the path of those who dislike paying fees is made all the easier. A young lady was admitted to the private wing of a London teaching hospital with a history of a throat infection which had led to a septicaemia and septic arthritis of the wrist. She was on the danger list for two days, after which she improved and the X-rays of the wrist taken on admission and those taken a week later, not surprisingly, revealed no abnormality. Twelve days after admission gentle movements of the wrist were ordered in an attempt to conserve some small range of active movement although it was appreciated that this could never be extensive. After a further few days the patient was discharged to attend the physiotherapy department, where two days later it was noted that the swelling had increased, and the registrar was consulted. He advised complete rest, and three days later the patient was seen again by the surgeon under whom she had been admitted, who advised that rest be continued and that she attend in a further four days for repeat X-rays.

The surgeon never saw his patient again and two days after her last attendance learned that she had been admitted to another hospital with a recurrence of the throat infection. Here, another surgeon was asked to see her but no contact was at any time made with his colleague. The X-rays taken at the teaching hospital were, however, on request forwarded to the hospital to which the patient had been admitted.

Repeated accounts were ignored by the patient and some months later her solicitors demanded a loan of the X-rays, so that they might advise their client regarding a possible action in negligence. The teaching hospital authorities pointed out that X-rays were normally lent solely to assist in the further treatment of a patient, but this merely resulted in a demand that the films be forwarded by return of post. This letter was treated strictly on its merits, that is to say ignored, but in point of fact the solicitors were in possession of the X-rays they were demanding, the second hospital having, without any reference to the first, forwarded the films which had been loaned to them.

This was the position when the surgeon sought advice regarding his fees and it was considered that here was a case where attack was the best method of defence. Demands for payment being ignored, a summons was issued which had the desired effect.

When one has a solicitor, or a member of his family, as a patient, it is but common prudence to take particular care, for one may be dealing with a patient who would not be slow to seek to take advantage of any shortcoming, real or apparent.

A solicitor patient attended a hospital casualty department complaining of a painful injury to his left calf which had occurred on the previous day. The casualty officer diagnosed a ruptured tendo-Achilles, and consulted the orthopaedic registrar regarding admission. The registrar advised that the foot be strapped and the patient be seen by the consultant orthopaedic surgeon the following week.

The consultant saw the patient in his clinic and decided that the plantaris tendon was ruptured but that a complete rupture of the tendo-Achilles was unlikely. He advised immobilisation in plaster and told the patient that the plaster would require to be left on for three weeks in the first place and possibly for a further three weeks after that. The next day a walking iron was fitted and the consultant told the patient that three weeks in plaster might be sufficient.

Two weeks later the registrar saw the patient and decided not to remove the plaster for a further fortnight. The patient was most disappointed and informed the nurse that he would not attend again. The same day he consulted another surgeon who diagnosed a complete rupture of the tendo-Achilles and advised immediate operation. The patient quickly made a claim against the hospital, and the hospital, with equal alacrity, passed the matter on to the surgeon's protection society. As it was not possible to find expert opinion to support the member's method of treatment, there was no choice but to explore a settlement which was finally achieved for a sum considerably below that originally claimed.

A case with a happier ending concerned a solicitor's wife who was admitted to a hospital in Scotland late one evening with an incomplete abortion, and the house surgeon performed a dilatation and curettage supervised by a senior house officer. Bleeding soon ceased and two days later the patient was discharged by the registrar. Three weeks after this the patient, having had a recurrence of vaginal bleeding for several days at home, was admitted to another hospital where a further dilatation and curettage was carried out and the consultant concerned noted that products of conception were removed. The day following this admission, the patient's husband wrote to the consultant under whom the patient had been admitted at the first hospital (although the consultant had not, in fact, ever seen the patient himself), and also wrote to the board of management claiming compensation for the pain and suffering undergone during the three weeks prior to admission to the second hospital which, he alleged, resulted from the negligence of the house surgeon. The view was taken that the house surgeon was justified both in her diagnosis and treatment, and that it is not necessarily negligent to fail to remove all products of conception. As regards the second hospital, surprise was expressed that products of conception were said to have been removed without histological examination. The patient's husband was then informed that any proceedings he might be minded to issue should be brought against the house surgeon and that the protection society's solicitors would be very pleased to accept service of the same. This led to a change in the direction of the attack, an attempt now being made to obtain further information by suggesting that, even were the house surgeon not negligent in the performance of the dilatation and curettage, she should not have undertaken it in the first place as the patient was only admitted for observation. The reply given to this was that there was nothing the society had to add to the previous correspondence and that was the last that was heard of the matter.

Similar problems can arise in general practice, as where, in an East Midland city, solicitors acting for a complainant wrote to the health authority alleging a long series of misdeeds on the part of the complainant's GP. According to the solicitors, he had repeatedly failed to visit, failed to examine, failed to diagnose, failed to treat, had demanded money from a National Health Service patient, and there was much more in this vein. For good measure a few allegations against the hospital were thrown in, one, in particular, stating that the patient was not properly examined. The solicitors stated that their letter was written as a result of the careful investigation they had carried out.

On going into the facts of the matter it soon appeared that almost every date the solicitors mentioned was incorrect. Their allegations against the GP were a travesty of the truth, and, regarding the hospital, the registrar concerned had, when faced with a patient admitted in coma on a Sunday evening, made the correct diagnosis of tuberculous meningitis and instituted treatment, albeit unsuccessfully. A reply sent to the authority was, as may be imagined, severely critical of the solicitors and made it clear that they could not have made any adequate investigation whatever. The matter was in due course referred to the Service Committee for hearing, and, their courtesy being apparently of the same order as their investigation, the solicitors and their client failed, without notice, to put in an appearance.

Evidence Against Colleagues

Doctors are, at times, approached by solicitors with a request that they support a claim alleging negligence against a professional colleague. Clearly if a doctor has been negligent and the patient has suffered harm thereby, medical evidence is going to be required before the plaintiff can succeed. There were, in the past, certain members of the profession who made a habit of appearing in such cases against colleagues, and presumably felt that the rewards compensated for any adverse opinion which their professional colleagues might hold regarding their activities. Occasionally odd references are made to the alleged difficulty of obtaining medical evidence in cases of professional negligence and it is claimed that there is a 'conspiracy of silence' in the profession. No such conspiracy is thought to exist, and when doctors so approached seek guidance from the Medical Protection Society, they are told that there is no objection to their giving a report and appearing as a witness should they feel it proper to do so, and that it is not thought that they will incur any ill-feeling within the profession, provided that they do not appear in this role with undue frequency and that they do not stray beyond their own field of competence. No doctor would wish that a patient who, through a doctor's negligence, had suffered real harm should go uncompensated for want of a medical witness. Where, however, solicitors try to get off the ground a case which, whatever its technical merits in law may be, is in the opinion of the vast majority of the medical profession entirely undeserving, then they will certainly have difficulty in finding a medical witness—which is a very good thing. The law was after all made for man. The solicitor may point out that it is not for the doctor to usurp the function of the Court and attempt to judge the merits of the case, but, granting this, the doctor is fully entitled to judge the morals and decide for himself whether, in all the circumstances, this is a case with which he would wish his name to be associated.

5 Coroners and Death Certification

The office of coroner tends to be regarded by some as a slightly ridiculous survival from a more or less distinguished past, having but little *raison d'être* in the twentieth century. Others see the coroner as an inquisitor, before whom they may be arraigned and, without the opportunity to speak in their defence, have their knowledge and actions subjected to public criticism. Extreme views are seldom either correct or helpful, and perhaps the best view is that the coroner system is as good as, but no better than, the coroner who administers it.

Time was when the office of coroner was one of great eminence, coroners having jurisdiction in criminal courts, and not the least of his duties being to ensure that the Crown became possessed of everything that rightly fell to it at a time when the goods of felons were forfeit, deodands passed to the Crown, and inquests on treasure trove, even allowing for the absence of banks and bank raids, occurred with a frequency which seems somewhat surprising. In the thirteenth and fourteenth centuries, when the coroner was at the peak of his eminence, the office was always filled by a knight possessed of lands, and the Statute of Westminster* had it that 'none but lawful most wise and discreet knights should be chosen'. The insistence on coroners being knights and owning land may have been, in part, a compliment to the office, but it was certainly an assurance that the Crown could, if need be, take action against the coroner should goods or monies be misappropriated, for in 1340 it was enacted that 'no coroner be chosen unless he had land in fee sufficient in the same county whereof he may answer to all manner of people'†.

That this was at times a necessary precaution is suggested by another ancient statute which reads, 'And forasmuch as mean persons and indiscreet now of late are commonly chosen to the

* 1235 (3 Edw. 3, c. 10). † 14 (Edw. 3, st. 1, c. 8).

office of coroner where it is requisite that persons honest, lawful and wise should occupy such offices'*.

With the institution of Justices of the Peace, the coroner's role in criminal cases came to an end and we learn from Blackstone that in the eighteenth century 'Through the culpable neglect of gentlemen of property this office has been suffered to fall into disrepute and get into low and indigent hands'. However low and indigent the coroner of that time may have been, it would seem that he must still have been possessed of land, for this requirement was not removed until the Coroners (Amendment) Act 1926, though it was said that certain coroners on appointment fulfilled their obligation in this respect by purchasing a grave plot.

Today coroners outside London are appointed by county authorities under the Local Government Act 1972 and in London by the Greater London Council. The only requirement is that they be registered medical practitioners, barristers, or solicitors, of not less than five years' standing. They are required to be, in person or by deputy, always available, and in England and Wales there are at present about 180 of whom only about 22 are full-time. Coroners are appointed for life and there can be few posts which carry such security of tenure, a point which tends to distress those who feel, rightly or wrongly, that they have been improperly attacked or criticised in the Coroner's Court. Unless he become a Sheriff, Alderman, or County Councillor, posts with which that of coroner is incompatible, a coroner can only be removed from office by the Lord Chancellor for neglect of duty or misconduct in the discharge of his duty. Even bankruptcy is not a ground for dismissal—the bankrupt coroner who was dismissed during the Second World War was dismissed essentially because he had disappeared without trace. Should a coroner—unthinkable perhaps in this country but it occurred not so long ago in a previous outpost of empire—be adjudged guilty of taking a bribe, of extortion, corruption, or of wilful neglect of duty, the Court of Trial may terminate his appointment.

Subject then to the above, to the power of the Attorney General to quash the coroner's inquisition, and to the Coroner's Rules, the coroner enjoys considerable freedom in respect of the exercise of his jurisdiction and over the proceedings in his court. He is entitled to judicial immunity regarding civil proceedings respecting acts done or words spoken in the exercise of his judicial duty, though such

* 3 Edw. 1 c. 10.

immunity would not apply were the acts done or words spoken in excess of or without jurisdiction. When the immunity applies it matters not that there was no reasonable cause nor even if it were proven that the coroner was activated by malice. The coroner has power to compel the attendance of witnesses under pain of fine or imprisonment for contempt, and under the Coroner's (Amendment) Rules 1980, certain persons are given the right to examine any witness either in person or by Counsel or solicitor. These persons include next-of-kin, beneficiaries under insurance policies, insurers, trade union representatives, inspectors appointed under the Health and Safety at Work Act 1974, and the Chief Officer of Police. The sub-section, however, which most concerns the doctor is that which includes any person whose act or omission may in the opinion of the coroner have caused or contributed to the death of the deceased. Any doctor finding himself in this situation should immediately seek legal representation through his protection society.

Notification to Coroner

There is, strange as it may seem, no legal duty on a doctor to notify the coroner of any death. There is, however, a common law duty on all those about a body to give notice to the coroner if it be thought that the deceased met his death from violence or unnatural means, or if it was a sudden death of unknown cause. There are, in addition, duties imposed upon Prison Governors to report all deaths of prisoners, and, as detailed later, the Registrar of Births and Deaths is required to report deaths occurring in specified circumstances.

The fact that there is no legal duty upon the doctor to notify the coroner of any death is, of course, not to be taken as implying that he need not do so when the circumstances require such action. Moral, ethical, and traditional considerations necessitate that the doctor acts with responsibility and, by notifying the coroner, facilitates such enquiry into the death as the coroner deems advisable. What circumstances then require a report to the coroner? In some cases, septic abortion, gunshot wounds, cut throat, the possibility that a serious crime has been committed, make the doctor's duty clear. Other cases are less definite and require more detailed consideration. Where a patient dies from injuries received in a recent accident the coroner should obviously be informed, but as time passes and the connection with the accident becomes more remote, the position becomes more difficult; there is little point in informing the coroner of the death of an elderly lady from bronchopneumonia several months after she became semi-bedridden following a fall in her home which resulted in a fractured neck of the femur. This would not constitute a violent or unnatural death nor a sudden death of unknown cause. Had the original injury resulted from a street accident, had the patient been a service pensioner and the injury perhaps connected with his pensionable disability, had the fall been in hospital or in the course of the patient's employment, were the relatives known to be critical of the medical or nursing treatment received, then in any of these circumstances the doctor might consider it advisable to report the death to the coroner.

What the doctor should not do is to ask the coroner whether he can sign a death certificate, for the coroner cannot give him any better authority than he already has. A doctor in attendance during the deceased's last illness is by statute* required to complete a death certificate giving the cause of death to the best of his knowledge and belief. The phrase 'during his last illness' is nowhere defined and can give rise to legitimate doubt; if one treats a patient for the first time during the last few moments of his life, is one in attendance during his last illness and therefore obliged to give a certificate? If one attends a patient with a peptic ulcer for a period, and six months later the patient, not having consulted another doctor in the interim, has a haematemesis and dies, should one give a certificate? The statute would seem so to require, but perhaps the better, and certainly the common sense view, is that in such cases the doctor is without the knowledge and belief required to complete the certificate.

To report to the coroner and to sign a death certificate are not of course mutually exclusive acts, for the certificate can be completed to show that the case has been reported to the coroner. When this is done the Registrar cannot register the death until the coroner notifies him of the result of his enquiries. However, to comply with the law the doctor should sign a death certificate where he has sufficient knowledge of the cause of death to do so, and in the following cases it is suggested that the coroner should be notified:

1 Violent deaths.
2 Sudden deaths where, though the terminal cause be known, the underlying causes are not.
3 Deaths from poisoning.
4 Deaths from industrial disease.
5 Deaths from drug addiction including alcoholism.

* Births and Deaths Registration Act 1953.

6 Deaths where there was no doctor in attendance.
7 Where doubt exists as to whether a child was live or stillborn.
8 Deaths resulting from abortion, therapeutic or criminal.
9 Deaths to which an accident has materially contributed.
10 Deaths which have been contributed to by an operation or anaesthetic, or where the operation and/or anaesthetic was necessitated by an injury.
11 Deaths of service pensioners or foster children.
12 Deaths where the patient's relatives have criticised the medical and/or nursing care provided for the patient.

The coroner derives his jurisdiction from the fact of a dead body lying in his area and, on being so informed, his enquiries are directed to determine four points: Who is this? How, when and where did he come by his death? The particulars required by the Registration Acts to be reported concerning the death.

The power of the coroner to indict for murder, manslaughter or infanticide was removed by the Criminal Law Act 1977. Where it appears that such crime has been committed by a known person the inquest is adjourned and a report made to the Director of Public Prosecutions.

Coroner's Investigation

The coroner will normally institute enquiries through his officer who is usually a serving policeman who conducts his duties in plain clothes, and it may be that on his reporting to the coroner the results of his interviews with relatives, doctors, and others, the coroner is satisfied that no further investigation is necessary. A doctor is under no obligation to answer the questions of the coroner's officer and, while it is usual for him to cooperate, it is entirely reasonable for him to seek advice before so doing. The coroner being satisfied, and a death certificate having previously been issued by the doctor in attendance during the deceased's last illness, the coroner completes Pink Form A, on receipt of which the Registrar registers the death in the terms of the certificate.

Alternatively, the coroner may decide that further investigation is required and he may order a post mortem or proceed directly to hold an inquest. There is a remarkable difference in the proportion of cases in which a post mortem is ordered in different parts of the country, and, in general, it would seem that the more populous the area, the more common are post mortems.

It is apparent that once one has notified the coroner of a death, or in any way become aware that the coroner is concerned in the matter, one must not proceed to arrange or conduct a post mortem, for to do so might be held to amount to obstructing the coroner in the execution of his duty. It is for the coroner to select the pathologist to perform the post mortem. While, when the death has occurred in hospital, this will usually be a pathologist connected with the hospital, in certain cases a pathologist with particular forensic experience may be chosen. Should there be any question of criticism of the medical or nursing care provided by the hospital, a pathologist from elsewhere will probably be asked to undertake the examination. Interested parties have, at the coroner's discretion, the right to be present or represented by a registered medical practitioner at the post mortem, though he must in no way interfere with the conduct of the examination. It is regrettable that doctors who have notified the coroner of a death are frequently not informed of the time and place of the subsequent post mortem.

The pathologist, following the post mortem, makes his report to the coroner who may then consider that no further enquiry is necessary, and in such cases he forwards to the Registrar Pink Form B showing the cause of death as found by the post mortem examination, on receipt of which the Registrar proceeds to register the death.

It is entirely for the coroner to determine whether to hold an inquest, and doctors sometimes too readily assume that such a decision implies that their conduct of the case is liable to be criticised. It should be appreciated that where there has been criticism the holding of an inquest may well, by bringing all the facts out into the open, make it clear that any criticisms expressed were entirely without foundation, and indeed, on occasion, the coroner may be at pains to state that the deceased received all possible care. In such cases the inquest may well have prevented the relatives of the deceased from pursuing a claim at civil law with all the worry and inconvenience that this would inevitably cause the doctor whatever the final result.

Where there is to be an inquest, the doctor in attendance on the deceased will likely have been asked for a report by the coroner's officer. Such report should be a detailed chronological account of the doctor's own part in the treatment of the patient, stating the days and, if relevant, the times the patient was seen, the history obtained, the diagnoses made, and the investigations and treatment ordered. It should not give the opinion of other doctors who, if need be, will be asked to report themselves; but where, for instance, a house officer has called in a registrar, he might report, 'I asked Dr X, the medical registrar, to see the patient and, subsequently, on his instructions I ordered an X-ray of the chest and gave an injection of (drug and dose)'. It is as well to retain a copy of one's report as a reminder of what precisely has been said, and if the doctor is proposing to contact his protection society with a view to their considering the provision of legal representation, he will certainly be asked for such a copy and he would be well advised to contact his society, by phone if need be, before the report is submitted.

The coroner is empowered to require the attendance of witnesses within his jurisdiction. When, then, the doctor is informed that he is required at the inquest he must, whatever the inconvenience, make the necessary arrangements to attend. Usually a message will be conveyed by the coroner's officer or, alternatively, a formal summons may be issued. Failure to appear—or refusal without lawful excuse to answer a question—can result in a fine being imposed or the witness being committed for contempt. Should attendance be impossible, e.g. when attending another court, or highly inconvenient, e.g. when abroad on holiday, a request for an adjournment will usually be sympathetically considered. The doctor should, on being asked to attend, give careful consideration as to whether in all the circumstances it is advisable for him to be legally represented. An inquest is of course an enquiry, not a trial, and as representation is the exception rather than the rule, it must be appreciated that the presence of a solicitor must to some extent cause other interested parties, and perhaps even the coroner, to wonder whether the doctor has something to fear or to hide.

A solicitor representing a witness in a Coroner's Court is in a very different position from one representing a client in a Magistrate's or County Court. He cannot address the coroner or the jury on matters of fact, though he may do so should any points of law arise, and his right to appear is entirely at the discretion of the coroner. The procedure is inquisitorial, as opposed to the accusatorial system of the criminal courts, and the witness is first examined by the coroner himself, following which the coroner may permit other interested parties, or Counsel or a solicitor representing such parties, to put questions to him. Finally, the witness's own legal representative may question him with a view to putting the evidence he has given in the most favourable light. Frequently, where other interested parties are legally represented the inquest is being regarded by them purely as an opportunity to obtain evidence on which to base a civil claim, and the witness might reasonably ask the coroner whether he is bound to answer such questions as appear to him not to be directed towards elucidating the facts which the inquest has been called to determine. Usually, the coroner can be depended upon not to permit irrelevant questions. Should, however, a witness consider that any answer he could give to a particular question would tend to incriminate him, as opposed to making him liable on a civil charge, he may decline to answer.

The main worry doctors have regarding inquests is that they may be unfairly criticised or criticised without the right to reply. Sometimes criticism may be made without the doctor even being present. Such cases are provided for by the provision in the Coroner's Rules*, that where the conduct of any person is called in question on grounds which the coroner thinks substantial, then the coroner shall adjourn the inquest to give that person the opportunity of being present unless the person concerned has been given prior notice of the inquest. A further safeguard is provided by the custom of permitting professional witnesses, and witnesses whose conduct may be called in question, to remain in Court throughout the proceedings, whereas other witnesses are excluded, except in non-contentious cases, until such time as they have given their evidence.

It may, however, occur that the doctor is present at an inquest and suddenly finds himself the target of attack by other interested parties. Let him first be sure that it is he himself who is the target. Relatives attending an inquest should be allowed a certain latitude, and if they let off a few blasts of hot air about doctors, nurses, hospitals, the National Health Service and anything else they happen to think of at the moment, then surely the doctor should have sufficient sympathy and charity to hope that the outburst has had a therapeutic effect. Once, however, a finger is pointed at him personally, the situation changes. The coroner will in all probability not permit such an attack to develop and will make it clear that his Court is not concerned with matters of civil liability. In the event, however, of the coroner not so intervening it is advised that the doctor should inform the coroner that he was unaware that an attack was to be made upon him, request an adjournment to enable him to obtain legal representation, and contact his protection society immediately.

Regarding evidence generally in a Coroner's Court, while the coroner has greater latitude in admitting statements than is the case in the criminal courts, this should not be taken to imply that any latitude is

* SI 1953 No. 205.

permitted on the part of witnesses. Best evidence, which might be loosely defined as first-hand evidence, is in general required, and there is seldom any excuse for a doctor appearing before the coroner to be in any doubt of the essential facts of the case, e.g. age, date of admission, date and time of operation, result of X-ray, and relevant pathological investigations, etc. The coroner will be justifiably irate regarding any such shortcoming on the part of a professional witness, who is after all being paid for his attendance.

The one point regarding evidence which is of particular concern to the doctor is that of dying declarations, for rare though these are, any doctor might at any time be called upon to take one. Before such a statement can be admitted, the patient must show that he understands that he is about to die and has no hope of recovery. Second, the statement must be about the manner in which he came to be in his present condition; and third, he must have died from the injuries or condition he described. The declaration may have been written down, possibly witnessed or even signed, or it may be given in oral evidence.

In the giving of evidence the doctor should, in the Coroner's Court as in every other Court, remember that simplicity and clarity will be appreciated. Even if the coroner is medically qualified, the jury and others interested in understanding what the doctor has to say are not. Where a doctor has given the matter adequate consideration before proceeding to the court, he will seldom find that it is not possible to explain what happened in everyday language—'oesophagoscopy resulted in an oesophagopleural fistula which led to a pyopneumothorax and mediastinitis' can more intelligibly be rendered as 'the wall of the gullet was damaged when the instrument was passed down to examine it and infection spread from there into the chest'. If anyone wishes to ask technical questions, well and good, but people do not like to feel that they are being blinded by science, or for that matter by legal or other technical jargon, and will respect the expert who can make his subject comprehensible.

The doctor should bring with him any necessary notes, should have a copy of his report, and, most important, should not try to give the impression that he knows more of the subject than he in fact does. A house officer is not expected to be an expert over the whole range of medicine and surgery, and, if asked for an opinion on a point regarding which he is uncertain, can reasonably say that as a house officer he does not feel qualified or able to assist the Court on that point. If he simply does not know the answer he should say so; it will certainly come out sooner or later and the sooner the better. There is usually nothing to be ashamed of in such an admission, for no doctor is expected to know everything.

There is, of course, no medical privilege in a Coroner's Court any more than there is in any other court. Should the doctor be asked a question regarding information which he acquired while in professional attendance on a patient, he may certainly point out to the coroner that he can only answer by divulging information obtained in the confidence of professional consultation, and ask whether he is bound to answer. Should the question be relevant the coroner will direct him to answer and the doctor would stand in contempt of Court should he refuse. He will, however, have made his position clear to the relatives and they will doubtless respect his solicitude on the deceased's behalf. Inquests are of course held in public, though no longer *super visum corporis*, and indeed the requirement that the coroner should view the body before he has jurisdiction was removed by the Coroners Act 1980. There are, from time to time, inquests held where there is no body, it having been totally destroyed, as by explosion, or being irrecoverable, as in cases of drowning or pit disasters.

The publicity given to an inquest by the Press can at times be unwelcome to the doctor, usually not so much from the content of the article as from the sensation-seeking headline. While many publications would appear to be oblivious to all considerations save the sale of their current edition, it must also be appreciated that, occasionally, some benefit to the public may emerge from reports of coroners' inquests. The usual example quoted is the Brides in the Bath case in 1915, when it was the report of the inquest on the third victim which led relatives of the first two to come forward and report the similarity in the manner in which the deaths had occurred. Police investigation then discovered that the husband was the same in each case and he was subsequently convicted of murder.

Coroners' Juries

The need for a jury in a Coroner's Court has been much reduced by the Criminal Law Act of 1977 and the Coroners (Amendment) Rules of the same year. Juries, who may number from seven to eleven, are now called where the coroner considers:

1 That death occurred in custody;

2 That the death occurred at work or on the railway;
3 That death occurred in circumstances the continuation of which are thought to be prejudicial to the health or safety of the public.

When he sits with a jury the normal procedure is for the coroner to sum up and direct the jury as to the law before they consider their verdict. Provided the minority does not exceed two, the coroner may accept a majority verdict. No riders may be added to the verdict, but the Coroners (Amendment) Rules 1980 permit the coroner to announce that he is reporting to the person or authority who may have power to take action to prevent similar fatalities.

The possible verdicts are: unlawful killing where the assailant is unknown, lawful killing, execution of sentence of death, lack of care or self-neglect, chronic alcoholism, addiction to drugs, want of attention at birth, stillborn, industrial disease, accident or misadventure, natural causes, abortion, suicide, and open. The verdict is seldom of particular interest to the doctor, for indeed the Coroners Rules expressly provide that no verdict shall be framed in such a way as to appear to determine any question of criminal liability on the part of a named person, or of civil liability. 'Want of attention at birth' would not be appropriate where there was thought to have been a 'lack of care'. It suggests rather that no one was available to give the necessary care. 'Lack of care' is in no way indicative of a fault by any particular person, and might well be used where any obligation was purely a moral one. 'Chronic alcoholism' and 'chronic addiction to drugs' are seldom used, for many addicts die from natural causes, and if from excess of alcohol or drugs, such excess may be accidental or possibly criminal. An open verdict implies that the evidence before the Court was inadequate to permit any other verdict being reached. Any interested party may apply for the Attorney General's fiat to quash the coroner's inquisition and a further inquest may be ordered.

Death Certification

The medical certificate of cause of death is an important document which should be completed with meticulous care. The book of certificates is perhaps a model of what a Government publication should be, for it sets out the statutory provisions governing medical certificates of the cause of death, includes helpful notes and suggestions to the certifying medical practitioner, a list of indefinite or undesirable terms, and also gives examples of how the certificates should be completed. It leaves, in short, no excuse for error nor reason for doubt, and the newly qualified would do well to study the information provided before first being called upon to complete a certificate. In saying that the book of certificates is excellent, this does not, of course, imply that the law itself is thought to be adequate in this matter. Perhaps the most glaring inadequacies are, first, there being no limit to the time during which the doctor must have seen the deceased prior to his death to entitle him to sign the death certificate, and, second, there being no requirement that the doctor view the body after death. Doctors are not meant to be detectives but they should have a healthy suspicion and not necessarily believe everything they are told. Can one really give a certificate with any degree of certainty unless one has seen the patient within a few days of his death? Because a patient suffers from a chronic disease which would be expected ultimately to cause his death, it does not follow that when he dies somewhat unexpectedly he died of that disease. Permanent invalids who make a considerable call on the services, time, and patience of others are not the least likely members of the community to be helped on their way out of this world. It may at times be difficult for the doctor to decline to give a certificate, but if he marks the certificate to the effect that he has reported the death to the coroner, the Registrar will delay registration until he receives the coroner's authority to proceed.

The examples given in the book of certificates make it immediately apparent that there is no point whatever in completing a certificate which contains a doubt; question marks and the word 'probably' have no place, for the Registrar must regard such cases as being deaths from unknown causes. It is appreciated that the full cause may not be known at the moment of death. If a hospital post mortem is to take place without undue delay, the certificate may with advantage be held over until this is completed, or, alternatively, the certificate may be completed showing that information from a post mortem examination may be available later. What cannot be approved is the obtaining of the relatives' permission for a post mortem by means of a threat to report the case to the coroner. If the case is one in which a report should be made to the coroner, then that report cannot properly be withheld by virtue of the relatives consenting to a post mortem. If the death does not necessitate reporting, then the relatives are within their rights in refusing permission for a post mortem, which then cannot take place unless the Registrar, being unable to accept the certificate completed to the best of the doctor's knowledge and belief, refers the matter to the coroner who then orders such examination. Very exceptionally, it may occur that a post mortem reveals some hitherto unknown condition which is thought to require a report to the coroner, and in such cases the examination should go no further until the coroner has been informed and his instructions obtained.

The Registrar is by regulations required to report to the coroner cases of the following nature:

1 Where no medical certificate of cause of death is produced.
2 Where the deceased has not been attended by a practitioner in his last illness.
3 Where the cause of death appears to be unknown.
4 Where the deceased was seen by a doctor neither after death nor within the fourteen days preceding death.
5 Where the Registrar considers that death may have resulted from violence, accident, or neglect.
6 Where death appears to have been due to abortion, industrial disease or poisoning.
7 Where death followed an operation necessitated by injury or occurred under an operation or before recovery from an anaesthetic.

The last of these circumstances is the one of particular interest to doctors, and it also raises a question on which there would appear to be a wide divergence of opinion between coroners. Where death occurs during or shortly after an operation, it would seem that some coroners take the view that as the operation possibly accelerated, if it did not cause, the death, then the death was an unnatural one or one resulting from violence, and therefore they invariably hold an inquest in such cases. Other coroners seem to take the view that, provided there has been no mishap regarding the conduct of the operation or anaesthetic, the patient died from the condition for which the operation was performed, i.e. death being from natural causes and no inquest being indicated. The essential difference between these two views is perhaps in the definition of the word 'unnatural', which the legislature may have intended to be defined as 'not in accordance with nature' but could equally have thought of as being equivalent to 'extraordinary' or 'unusual'. While the surgeon might very reasonably resent being called to an inquest when his patient has died on the table, taking the view that had he died before the operation started or had he, the surgeon, decided that the case was inoperable, he would not have been troubled, he should also realise that the inquest may have the effect of allaying any doubts the deceased's relatives may have, and thereby avoiding subsequent criticism which could prove much more time-consuming than the inquest.

Some coroners have sought to bring pressure on hospitals to report all deaths occurring within twenty-four or forty-eight hours of admission and/or operation. Not withstanding the need, in the interests of the relatives of the deceased, for the hospital and doctors to cooperate with the coroner, it cannot be thought that such a demand, which has no legal sanction, is reasonable or indeed satisfactory. Cases vary to such an extent that no such arbitrary rule can be always appropriate, and the list of cases in which a report to the coroner is thought to be advisable will perhaps provide a more satisfactory basis, while leaving the final decision where it belongs, namely, in the hands of the doctor in each particular case.

Brain Death

There is no legal definition of death. A person is therefore dead when a doctor says he is dead. Sometimes the doctor will be in doubt. He will then maintain circulation and respiration by artificial means until such time as he is satisfied that brain death—or perhaps more accurately brain stem death—has occurred. He may indeed at the request of the patient's relatives maintain the support systems for a while longer knowing full well that all he is doing is ventilating a corpse.

When then the doctor comes to complete documentation regarding the date and time of death he should state this to the best of his knowledge and belief. The time when the support systems were discontinued is irrelevant, and indeed to insert this as the time of death suggests a causative connection. It may be that the doctor comes to consider that the patient was dead on admission. It may be that the time when examination failed to elicit evidence of brain stem function is thought to be the most accurate estimation that can be made. As in cases of death where no support systems have been used, the doctor should carefully consider all the available evidence and give his best opinion. Much may depend upon his decision.

There are two authoritative statements on the issue of brain death. That of the World Medical Association is encapsulated in the Declaration of Sydney and appears in Appendix A on page 194.

The second is a memorandum issued by the Honorary Secretary of the Conference of Medical Royal Colleges and their Faculties in the United Kingdom in 1979, and runs as follows:

1 In October 1976 the Conference of Royal Colleges and their Faculties (UK) published a report unanimously expressing the opinion that 'brain death', when it had occurred, could be diagnosed with certainty. The report has been widely accepted. The conference was not at that time asked whether or not it believed that death itself should be presumed to occur when brain death takes place or whether it would come to some other conclusion. The present report examines this point and should be considered as an addendum to the original report.
2 Exceptionally, as a result of massive trauma, death occurs instantaneously or near-instantaneously. Far more commonly, death is not an event: it is a process, the various organs and systems supporting the continuation of life failing and eventually ceasing altogether to function, successively and at different times.
3 Cessation of respiration and cessation of the heart beat are examples of organic failure occurring during the process of dying, and since the moment that the heart beat ceases is usually detectable with simplicity by no more than clinical means, it has for many centuries been accepted as the moment of death itself, without any serious attempt being made to assess the validity of this assumption.
4 It is now universally accepted, by the lay public as well as by the medical profession, that it is not possible to equate death itself with the cessation of the heart beat. Quite apart from the elective cardiac arrest of open-heart surgery, spontaneous cardiac arrest followed by successful resuscitation is today a common-place and although the more sensational accounts of occurrences of this kind still refer to the patient being 'dead' until restoration of the heart beat, the use of the quote marks usually demonstrates that this word is not to be taken literally, for to most people the one aspect of death that is beyond debate is its irreversibility.
5 In the majority of cases in which a dying patient passes through the processes leading to the irreversible state we call death, successive organic failures eventually reach a point at which brain death occurs and this is the point of no return.
6 In a minority of cases brain death does not occur as a result of the failure of other organs or systems but as a direct result of severe

damage to the brain itself from, perhaps, a head injury or spontaneous intracranial haemorrhage. Here the order of events is reversed: instead of the failure of such vital functions as heart beat and respiration eventually resulting in brain death, brain death results in the cessation of spontaneous respiration; and this is normally followed within minutes by cardiac arrest due to hypoxia. If, however, oxygenation is maintained by artificial ventilation the heart beat can continue for some days, and haemoperfusion will for a time be adequate to maintain function in other organs, such as the liver and kidneys.

7 Whatever the mode of its production, brain death represents the state at which a patient becomes truly dead, because by then all functions of the brain have permanently and irreversibly ceased. It is not difficult or illogical in any way to equate this with the concept in many religions of the departure of the spirit from the body.

8 In the majority of cases, since brain death is part of or the culmination of a failure of all vital functions, there is no necessity for a doctor specifically to identify brain death individually before concluding that the patient is dead. In a minority of cases in which it is brain death that causes failure of other organs and systems, the fact that these systems can be artificially maintained even after brain death, has made it important to establish a diagnostic routine which will identify with certainty the existence of brain death.

Conclusion

9 It is the conclusion of the conference that the identification of brain death means that the patient is dead, whether or not the function of some organs, such as a heart beat, is still maintained by artificial means.

Cremation

Consideration of the various forms will perhaps give the clearest outline of the law's requirements in the matter of cremation.

Form A is the application for cremation, usually completed by a relative whose signature the doctor may be requested to witness.

Form B is the first medical certificate to be completed by a practitioner who has attended the deceased during his last illness and who can certify definitely as to the cause of death. Provisionally registered practitioners may sign this form.

Form C is the confirmatory medical certificate, given occasionally by the Medical Referee, but usually by any practitioner fully registered for not less than five years, who must not be a relative of the deceased nor a relative or partner of the doctor who has signed the certificate in Form B. Difficulties arise regarding this reference to 'partner', and it would seem that the regulation was drafted with general rather than hospital practice in mind. What is clearly intended is that the doctor signing the confirmatory certificate should be independent of the doctor who signed the certificate in Form B. It cannot, therefore, be thought proper for a houseman and registrar on the same firm to sign the two certificates, and the Medical Referee might reasonably refuse to accept such certificate. A fee is payable for the signing of the confirmatory certificate both in hospital and general practice, and problems can arise as to who in hospital practice has the right to nominate the doctor to sign this certificate. The answer must be that, as the consultant under whose care the patient was has the duty of seeing that Form B is completed either personally or by his registrar or houseman, he also has the responsibility for arranging for the completion of Form C, which duty again he may delegate to his juniors. However, cases may occur where the patient is not attended by the consultant, and then it is for the doctor who attended the patient in his last illness to sign Form B and arrange for a suitable colleague to sign the confirmatory certificate. The need for a confirmatory certificate has recently been questioned, and it certainly has no value unless a complete external examination is carried out. This may not please the undertaker, mortuary attendant, or whoever has the care of the body, but the requirements of the Cremation Regulations are not complied with by casting an eye on an enshrouded and coffined corpse as one is often, by implication at least, invited to do. It is further necessary that one sees and questions the doctor who signed the certificate in Form B, and it has been stated that a telephonic communication is insufficient.

Form D is a certificate given following a post mortem carried out by a pathologist appointed by the coroner or by the Medical Referee.

Form E, an alternative to either Forms B and C, or Form D, is a certificate given by a coroner following a post mortem examination or an inquest.

Form F is the authority to cremate given by the Medical Referee upon his being satisfied that the necessary forms are in order, that the cause of death has been definitely ascertained, and that the coroner is not proposing to hold an inquest.

Form G is the Register of Cremations kept by the Cremation Authority.

Criticism by Coroner

Much has been said of the duty of the doctor to give all reasonable cooperation and help to the coroner and it is regrettable, to put it mildly, when a doctor finds himself subjected to unreasonable criticism and treated with scant courtesy by a coroner. There are perhaps very few hospital residents, and indeed few of their seniors, who would anticipate fatal or serious results from the ingestion of half an ounce of gentian violet solution which was known to have been prescribed for topical application. In this case, the patient in question, aged eighty-two, was brought to a casualty department having been found with blue stains around her mouth. An examination by two residents proving negative except for the existence of a cardiac murmur, the patient was permitted to return home but died about half an hour after leaving the hospital. Statements were given to the coroner's officer and nothing further was heard by the doctors until they were given about four and a half hours' notice of their attendance being required at an inquest. Representation was hurriedly arranged, but clearly time precluded adequate information being obtained and full instructions being given.

The coroner, presumably unaware of the rarity of gentian violet poisoning, took it upon himself to enquire at embarrassing length into the qualifications of one of the doctors and, in his summing up, made critical references to foreign doctors with little experience of English people, being permitted to work without supervision. These remarks, unfortunate and embarrassing as they were, did not permit of any action being taken, but a courteous letter was addressed to the coroner by solicitors representing the doctor's protection society. This pointed out the inadequate notice given and added that, where there was any likelihood of a doctor's qualifications and competence being criticised, it was considered to be of the utmost importance that the doctor's advisers should have reasonable opportunity of investigating the facts and taking advice on technical matters. The coroner was asked for his assurance that this situation would not be repeated.

The attitude of this coroner was made very clear by his reply which referred to the solicitors' letter as instructing him as to how he should carry out his duty, enclosed a report from the police and said that he was not prepared to discuss the matter further. The police report stated that prior to the notice being given to the doctors a verbal message had, several days before, been left with a sister in the hospital. The only reasonable assumption from the nature of the coroner's reply would seem to be that he was seeking to reject what he knew to be a legitimate complaint regarding the practice he employed. However, despite the tone of his letter, there is reason to think that doctors in his district have not been so discourteously treated since this incident.

Fees

No fee is payable to a doctor for notifying a death to a coroner. Should a doctor be asked to supply a report to the coroner, most local authorities authorise a fee, though the actual sum in each case may be subject to the coroner's discretion. The story is told of one very short and illegible report being rewarded with the amount the coroner estimated would purchase the doctor a cheap brand of pen!

Medical witnesses in Coroners' Courts and practitioners performing post mortems are remunerated according to the Coroners (Fees and Allowances) Rules as amended. At the time of writing, in 1981, the following notes apply:

1 (i) A medical practitioner who makes a post mortem examination of a body by the coroner's direction or at the coroner's request and reports the result thereof to the coroner and who is not a witness at an inquest on that body shall be paid a fee of £26.05.
(ii) A medical practitioner who makes a post mortem examination of a body by the coroner's direction or at the coroner's request and reports the result thereof to the coroner and who is a witness at an inquest on that body shall be paid a fee of £41.60 in respect of the examination and of the first day of which he attends to give evidence at the inquest and in addition a further fee of £20.80 for each subsequent day on which he attends to give evidence at the inquest; provided that if he attends to give evidence at more than one inquest held on the same day on the bodies of persons whose deaths appear to have been caused by the same accident or occurrence, he shall be paid a fee of £26.05 in respect of the post mortem examination of each such body made by him and in addition a fee of £20.80 in respect of each day on which he attends to give evidence at such inquests.
(iii) A medical practitioner who is a witness at an inquest shall, for attending to give professional evidence otherwise than in connection with a post mortem examination made by him at the coroner's direction or at the coroner's request, be paid a fee of £20.80 for

each day on which he attends to give evidence at the inquest; provided that if he attends to give evidence at more than one inquest held on the same day, he shall be paid a fee of £12.90 in respect of his attendance at each inquest held on that day other than the first.

2 A witness practising as a member of the legal profession or as a dentist or veterinary surgeon may, for attending to give professional evidence whether at one or more inquests, be paid a professional witness allowance not exceeding £31.75 per day; provided that if the witness attends on any day to give evidence at one inquest only and the period during which he is necessarily absent from his place of residence or practice to attend as aforesaid does not exceed four hours, his professional witness allowance shall not exceed £15.90, unless he necessarily incurs expense in the provision for the occasion of a person to take care of his practice during his absence.

3 An expert witness at any inquest may, for attending to give expert evidence and for work in connection with its preparation, be paid an expert witness allowance of such amount as the coroner may consider reasonable having regard to the nature and difficulty of the case and the work necessarily involved.

Transplants

Where the circumstances require that a death be reported to the coroner, no organ or tissue may be removed without his consent as required by the Human Tissue Act 1961. This consent does not, of course, do away with the need for authorisation by the person in lawful possession of the body.

6 Criminal Law

It is not the intention here to attempt to refer to all the possible crimes of which a doctor could be accused, but merely to those in respect of which the very nature of his profession renders him particularly vulnerable.

Criminal Abortion

Every clinician must at some time or other have been asked for help by a patient desirous of having her pregnancy terminated. It may be that the request is for 'something to regulate the periods' or some such euphemism, but it is essential that whatever the doctor does he makes it apparent to the patient beyond all shadow of doubt that he is not helping to cause an unlawful abortion. The writer has painful memories of a patient returning with tangible signs of her deep gratitude for the 'wonderful pills which made everything all right'. What had happened in fact was that the patient had been told quite firmly that a doctor could not do anything to help bring about an abortion without there being adequate cause, but at the same consultation some tablets had been prescribed for her cold. It was evident that the patient had no doubt that the tablets had terminated her pregnancy, and the fact that her cold was precisely the same as before must have lent support to her conviction. For some weeks the writer was afraid that she might make recommendation to her friends and relations but, fortunately, she proved to be a tactful as well as a grateful patient and, as far as is known, never divulged what, no doubt, she regards to this day as a secret between us.

The Abortion Act 1967 changed the entire legal framework of the subject. The first essential to appreciate is that termination of a pregnancy, except in accordance with the provisions of the Act, is unlawful and constitutes a criminal offence under the Offences against the Person Act 1861.

Circumstances Permitting Termination of Pregnancy

The Act provides that a person shall not be guilty of an offence under the law relating to abortion when a pregnancy is terminated by a registered medical practitioner, if two registered medical practitioners are of the opinion, formed in good faith:

1 That continuation of the pregnancy would endanger the life of the pregnant woman or
2 That continuation of the pregnancy would involve risk to the physical or mental health of the pregnant woman greater than if the pregnancy was terminated or
3 That continuation of the pregnancy would involve injury to the physical or mental health of any existing children of the pregnant woman's family greater than if the pregnancy was terminated or
4 That there exists a substantial risk that if the child were born it would suffer from such physical or mental abnormalities as to be seriously handicapped.

The Act also provides that in determining whether the continuance of a pregnancy would involve such risk to the health of the pregnant woman or of her existing children, account may be taken of her actual or reasonably foreseeable environment.

Unless the case falls within one or more of the four above-mentioned sets of circumstances and termination of the pregnancy is carried out under the conditions mentioned in the Act, such termination will be unlawful.

Duties of Certifying Practitioners

A practitioner before certifying should give careful consideration to all the relevant circumstances which might bring his patient in to one of the four categories. This may necessitate obtaining information regarding her personal and family physical and mental history, her social history and condition, details of her existing family and any abnormal stresses and strains thereon, and details of any circumstances, virus infections, drug taking, etc., which might be thought likely to lead to a seriously handicapped child being born. To reach an opinion, a doctor may need to make enquiries of other doctors, social workers, children's officers, probation officers, and others.

A practitioner who declines to recommend a patient for abortion solely on the grounds of conscientious objection is strongly advised to refer the patient to a colleague.

Definitions

Counsel's opinion has been obtained as to the meaning and construction which the courts are likely to place on certain words and phrases in the Act, and the views expressed by Counsel are as follows:

> 'injury to the physical or mental health of . . . any existing children of her family.'

'Children'
This term would include a single child and might, in exceptional circumstances of dependency, include a person over the age of twenty-one.

'Children of Her Family'
Counsel considers this term not to be restricted to the legitimate children to whom the pregnant woman has given birth, but to include adopted and illegitimate children of herself or her husband. Exceptionally, other children such as brothers and sisters of an unmarried pregnant woman living in family with her might be included. The test is thought to be the child's dependency upon the pregnant woman.

> 'that there is a substantial risk that if the child were born it would suffer from such physical or mental abnormalities as to be seriously handicapped.'

'Substantial'
A substantial risk must be more than a mere possibility. It must be a risk of a degree which merits serious consideration. Providing the two certifying practitioners, in good faith, decide that the risk is substantial, it is not considered that they would stand in any appreciable danger of prosecution on this point.

'Seriously Handicapped'
Counsel has suggested that a child may be considered seriously handicapped if unlikely to be able to live an independent life when of an age to do so.

'Treatment'
Treatment authorised by the Act must normally be carried out in an NHS hospital, or in a place approved for the purpose by the Secretary of State.

Examination by a certifying practitioner is not considered to be 'treatment' within the meaning of the Act, and therefore need not be carried out in any particular place. Where treatment is immediately necessary to save the life or to prevent grave permanent injury to the physical or mental health of the pregnant woman, it may be carried out elsewhere than in an NHS hospital or approved place. In such circumstances no second opinion is required.

Duties of Practitioner Undertaking Termination

The practitioner undertaking termination will frequently be one of the certifying practitioners but this is not obligatory.

Disagreement on Clinical Indications

Although two practitioners have certified that circumstances justify termination according to Section 1(1), a gynaecologist might not consider termination to be clinically indicated. Ethically, he cannot act contrary to what he believes to be the patient's best interests. In such circumstances, it is suggested that in fairness to the patient, and for his own protection, he advise and assist her to obtain a further opinion through her general practitioner.

Conscientious Objection

Section 4(1) of the Act states that no person shall be under any duty, whether by contract or by any statutory or other legal requirement, to participate in any treatment authorised by the Act to which he has a conscientious objection. It adds that in any legal proceedings, the burden of proof of conscientious objection shall rest on the person claiming to rely on it.

It is considered that a doctor will have little difficulty in establishing a valid conscientious objection if he can show the sincerity of his belief that participation in an abortion, either (*a*) under any circumstances or (*b*) in the circumstances of a particular case, would offend against his own concept of what is right or wrong.

In Scotland, the doctor has in any legal proceedings but to make a statement on oath that he has a conscientious objection to participate in any treatment authorised by the Act to establish his position.

Section 4(2) states that Section 4(1) shall not affect any duty to participate in treatment necessary to save the life or to prevent grave permanent injury to the physical or mental health of a pregnant woman. As a doctor has an obvious duty in such cases, the defence that he had a conscientious objection would not be available in any subsequent proceedings.

Documentation

Regulations made under the Act impose upon practitioners duties respecting documentation. Forms are prescribed for certifying practitioners and for the notification of the termination of the pregnancy. Preservation and disposal of the required certificates, time limits within which these must be completed and forwarded, and restrictions on the disclosure of information, are also covered.

Practitioners are advised to use scrupulous care in respect of the matters, and it is stressed that failure to comply with the requirements constitutes an offence which can result in a fine of up to £100.

Consent to Operation

Parent's Consent (daughter sixteen to eighteen years of age)
A parent's consent in such cases is desirable but not legally necessary. Such a patient is, in general, entitled to professional secrecy and, therefore, parental consent should seldom be sought against her will.

Each case must be considered on its merits—there is an obvious difference between two seventeen-year-old girls, one a pupil at a boarding school and the other maintaining herself away from the parental home. The age at which consent may be given for medical treatment is dealt with on page 106, and abortion is not essentially different from other operations or therapy.

Parent's Consent (daughter aged under sixteen)
An approach to a parent or guardian should be made wherever possible.

Husband's/Father's Consent
The views of the lawful husband should be considered. Such views cannot, however, prevent an operation considered necessary 'to save the life or prevent grave permanent injury' to the mother. The

consent of a common law husband or putative father is not necessary in law.

Where the indications for abortion concern the health of 'the pregnant woman or any existing children of her family' the husband's views are but one aspect to be considered when taking account of 'the pregnant woman's actual or reasonably foreseeable environment'.

Emergencies must not, of course, await upon consent.

Penalties

Any doctor who is convicted of any offence concerned with the procuring of an abortion must anticipate both imprisonment and erasure from the Register; yet in spite of these dire penalties, cases *do* occur and occasionally come to light through the most unexpected channels. Lest any reader at any time be tempted to think that a matter which both doctor and patient will wish to keep quiet about must therefore be fairly safe, a case which occurred some years ago and led to a doctor's appearance at the Old Bailey and, subsequently, before the Disciplinary Committee of the General Medical Council, when his name was duly erased from the Register, is herewith mentioned. It was not disputed that the doctor had seen and examined the girl. While the nature of his examination procedure was not agreed, and was of the essence so far as his guilt or otherwise was concerned, the cautionary aspect of the case lies in what occurred when the girl subsequently aborted. The man with whom she was living took the fetus, wrapped it in brown paper and carried it down a fire escape at the back of the flats where they lived, placing the parcel in the dustbin. The dustcart was apparently collecting in the street at the time and the contents of the bin were duly dumped aboard. The cart was somewhat loaded and the brown paper parcel fell off and rolled into the gutter opening as it did so to reveal the fetus. One of the dustmen, being of an observant nature, recollected seeing the parcel being brought down the fire escape, identified the flat from which it had come, and informed the police. The rest followed.

Role of Nurses

Abortion by the extra amniotic infusion of prostaglandins was not envisaged when the Abortion Act was framed. The Royal College of Nursing sought to assert that nurses should not take part in the procedure on the grounds that by injecting prostaglandins they were terminating pregnancy, a function reserved by the Act to registered medical practitioners. The case Royal College of Nursing *v* Department of Health & Social Security* came before the House of Lords, where the decision was that where the termination was decided upon by a registered medical practitioner who remained responsible for the procedure, he was not required to carry out every part of it, and a nurse acting on a doctor's instructions was not acting illegally.

Abortion Law Reform

Repeated attempts to amend the Abortion Act have come to nought, mainly owing to the extreme positions taken up by the pro- and anti-abortion lobbies which have resulted in stalemate. The main area of public concern surrounds late terminations where the birth of a viable fetus is possible.

The Abortion Act itself states, 'Nothing in the Act shall affect the provisions of the Infant Life (Preservation) Act 1929'. The 1929 Act states that where the pregnancy has lasted for 28 weeks, that is *prima facie* proof that the child was capable of being born alive. Anyone who with intent causes such a child to die before it has an existence independent of its mother may under this Act be convicted of the offence of child destruction.

No Act says that a child born earlier than 28 weeks is presumed not to be capable of being born alive, and should a fetus show any sign of life, then, irrespective of the duration of the pregnancy, the doctor's duty is precisely the same as that which he owes to any new born babe under his care.

With advances in the care of premature infants the chances of survival at 24 weeks or even earlier must increase, and as they do, so must the consideration given by the doctor, prior to advising abortion at this stage of pregnancy.

Indecent Assault

Every doctor in clinical practice must at all times be on his guard against allegations of indecent assault being made against him. It is all very well to say, 'Never examine a woman without a chaperon

* NLJ (*New Law Journal*) Feb. 12 1981, page 176.

being present', but this is the counsel of perfection not of practicability. It is not always that the ward sister can, and will, release a nurse to chaperon a houseman. Should examination without a chaperon then be necessary, the screen should not be too closely drawn, the doctor should explain the purpose of his examination in a voice loud enough to be heard by at least two nearby patients and vaginal examination should only be undertaken in emergency. Even when a chaperon is obtained, danger still exists. How common it is to find that something is missing and the nurse is asked to fetch the sphygmomanometer or the patella hammer. 'He sent the nurse away' can be made to sound much more sinister than if the nurse had never been there in the first place, and these words very commonly appear in a complainant's allegation. It is usually better to collect whatever it is oneself or, otherwise, to spend the time the nurse is away taking a further history standing by a gap in the screen.

What happens if a complaint is made? Perhaps the allegation is that the patient was complaining of a pain in the foot and the doctor fondled her breasts. It is seldom that the complaint is made immediately after the alleged assault and it may be made to the police or to the hospital authority. The doctor may then be summoned to the administrator's office or asked to call at the police station. He is told very briefly what the complaint is and asked for his observations. At this moment he is faced with two sources of danger; the minor source the patient, and the major source his own big mouth. The position is that the police or hospital authority have, at that time, an uncorroborated story of an alleged assault. No corroboration is possible in the vast majority of cases and the police know perfectly well that, in such cases, every Judge will stress how dangerous it is to rely on an uncorroborated allegation of this nature. Therefore, they are most unlikely to prefer a charge unless the doctor helps them. Provided then that he wishes to deny the allegations he should say, 'I most strongly deny that anything other than a normal examination took place', and to the next question, whatever it may be, he replies 'I have nothing further to say'. He then shuts up, and stays silent, and rings his protection society at the first opportunity. In all probability nothing further will be heard from the police and, if a hospital enquiry is ordered, his protection society will be pleased to help.

However, what does often occur? The doctor in reply to the policeman's first question denies the assault. The policeman is very affable and oozes confidence and reassurance. He just wishes to get this little matter cleared up for everyone's sake. 'I see, doctor,' he says, 'it was just a normal examination; but tell me, how do you think the patient came to imagine that there was something improper about it?' 'I don't know what she thought,' the doctor replies somewhat sharply. 'No, quite,' says the policeman, 'I appreciate that, but you are not telling me, are you, that the patient has made up this whole story just to cause trouble? I mean, you do accept that she must have thought, however mistakenly, that something wasn't quite right or she wouldn't have come to us, would she?' 'I suppose not. I suppose she must have misunderstood what was happening,' the doctor confesses in support of his patient, and quite oblivious of the harm he is doing to his own interests. 'Well then,' the policeman proceeds, 'I wonder how she got the wrong end of the stick. Did you explain to her exactly what you were doing?' 'Well it was just an ordinary examination of the chest. It didn't call for an explanation.' 'But she was complaining of her foot.' 'Yes, but every patient has a full examination. The pain in the foot might have been rheumatic so I had to examine the heart.' 'I see that, but the fact is, is it not, that this patient did not know that there was any reason for an examination of her chest? You have told me that you did not explain the need to her, and she is now saying that she did not consent to such an examination, which she therefore claims was an assault and perhaps an indecent assault.' Some days later the doctor is served with a Summons, the matter goes to the Magistrate's Court and from there to the Crown Court where, if all goes well for the doctor, the Judge refers to the lack of corroboration and the doctor is found not guilty. He has had weeks of worry and anxiety and it need never have happened. He talked his way into it. Incredible as it may seem, doctors seem to be so naive that they go through all this interrogation by the police and still think that the police are trying to do them a favour. One doctor, while awaiting the commencement of his trial at the Old Bailey, said to the writer that the police had been very nice and had even rung him that morning to wish him good luck. It had never occurred to him that the police had wanted to make sure that he was at home and was going to appear.

Occasionally, however, a patient's complaints will be such that the police will proceed despite the doctor's denials. A senior house officer in the accident and orthopaedic department of a hospital was asked to examine a girl aged eighteen who complained of pain in the left side of her chest following a fall downstairs at her home the previous day. At his request, the girl removed the top part of her clothing and he carried out an examination of the left ribs. The girl complained in addition of pain in the right hip, left shoulder and over the right eye and these parts were also duly examined. Shortly afterwards the patient complained to members of the hospital staff that the doctor had improperly handled her breasts and kissed her. These allegations were denied by the house officer, first when they were put to him by the medical administrator, second when in the presence of the girl and her boy friend he was asked for an apology for his conduct and refused to give one, and third when interviewed by the police. He was, nevertheless, charged with indecent assault and, at the preliminary hearing, was advised to elect to go for trial by jury, and he was duly committed to the higher court where he pleaded 'not guilty'.

The girl said in evidence that after examining her ribs the doctor put his hand out and 'nipped hold of' her left breast and that he then caught hold of both her breasts and 'squeezed them'. She further stated that while he was examining her eye he had put his hand behind her head and kissed her and tried to force his tongue into her mouth. Evidence was given by members of the hospital staff that shortly after the examination the girl had complained of the doctor's conduct and that she then appeared to be distressed and was crying. A staff nurse and the assistant receptionist who had entered the room separately at two different stages while the girl was being examined agreed that what they observed appeared to be part of a perfectly proper examination. In his own evidence, the doctor said that he had examined each of the left ribs in turn down to the fifth rib. In doing so it had been necessary to palpate the left breast and to lift up the breast in order to feel the fourth and fifth ribs. When he had got as far as the fifth rib the girl had turned away, muttered something inaudible, dressed quickly, and left the room. He denied touching the girl's breasts at all, except to the extent he had previously stated, and he completely denied the allegation of having kissed her. The medical administrator who was called as a witness by the prosecution spoke very highly of the doctor's character and ability.

In his summing up, the Chairman warned the jury of the dangers of convicting on a charge of this nature, unless the evidence of the complainant was corroborated. He also stressed the semi-public nature of the room in which the examination took place, in that nursing staff frequently came in and out of a door giving access to the patients' waiting hall, and there was a hatchway communicating with the adjoining treatment room which was often open and could be opened at any time from the other side. The Chairman further reminded the jury of the defendant's consistent denials of the allegations right from the start. After a short retirement the jury brought in a verdict of 'not guilty'.

A second example, this time from abroad, concerned a recently established gynaecologist who conducted a post-natal examination without a nurse being present, and finding a copious vaginal discharge, took a specimen of this with the patient in the lithotomy position. He concluded his examination and, there being some vulval irritation due to the discharge, he applied a steroid preparation to the vulva, an action which was no doubt imprudent, to say the least. The patient reacted by shouting at him to 'get out' and subsequently contacted the police alleging, indeed, that she had felt what seemed to her like a male organ at the vulva. Her husband phoned the doctor later that evening stating that he was coming around to murder him, at which point the doctor became quite incapable of logical thought and behaved in an extraordinary manner. He left his house, leaving his family to cope with the patient's husband if he called on his homicidal mission, drove for several miles, took a quantity of barbiturates, went to a hotel, slashed his wrists and woke up in hospital three days later to find a policeman at his bedside.

By the time this case reached the stage where the Magistrate was saying how dangerous it was to accept the uncorroborated story of a patient in a case such as this, and making it perfectly plain that he held a very low opinion of both the character and the veracity of the patient in question, the defence costs had become substantial. While the doctor's conduct certainly appears to have been odd, perhaps those of us who have not faced such a situation should be slow to criticise. On the other hand, it can hardly be thought that the police would have prosecuted had the doctor firmly denied the allegations, and pointed out that no doctor could reasonably be thought to have contemplated intercourse with a woman with a copious vaginal discharge of uncertain aetiology.

Assault

Common assault is defined as an attempted battery; that is an attempt to offer to do a corporal hurt to another even without touching him as when the fist is raised in a threatening manner. Although the person assaulted need not be actually touched, mere words can never constitute an assault. From this it follows that it is an asssault to carry out any examination or treatment which involves laying a finger on the patient without consent. Precisely the same considerations regarding consent apply as in civil law, and the problem is discussed in the chapter on that subject.

Assault by Doctor

When patients allege assault they almost invariably prefer civil to criminal proceedings as their desire is to make all possible profit from what has been, in the vast majority of cases, nothing more than an error made in all good faith, but occasionally the doctor finds himself in the Magistrate's Court. The usual circumstance having this result is that a practitioner on the impulse of the moment slaps a child. Dental anaesthetists whose fingers are bitten are on occasion apt to fetch the youthful patient a sharp backhander across the face, unfortunately accompanied at times with a few expletives concerning, perhaps, the child's parentage. In such circumstances there are two defences open to the practitioner. First it can be said that the slap was therapeutic—the child was behaving in an hysterical manner and the treatment for hysteria is a sudden sharp shock, administered in this case as a slap. Alternatively, it can be put forward that the doctor regarded himself as being *in loco parentis*; he knew the family very well and felt sure that the parents would wish that he should so control the child, as indeed they would themselves had they been present, to enable the necessary dental treatment to be carried out. Both these defences can sound very well on occasion, but they accord only with that carefully considered and meticulously meted out chastisement which is, of course, the only type which those of us who are parents have ever awarded to our own children. When, however, the little devil (horns now exchanged for angel's wings) peeps over the witness box and is asked, 'And did the man say anything before he slapped you?' and replies, 'Yes, he called me a b . . . . . little b . . . .' then clearly there are storms ahead.

Assault on Doctor

There was a time in the lives of us all when the word 'patient' was inevitably preceded by the adjective 'grateful'. We imagined that the doctor's life must, whatever its hardships, be one of pleasure and serenity, for indeed, what man could expect to receive in like measure the gratitude and esteem of all with whom he came into contact in his daily round? For most of us these fond dreams evaporated prior to qualification, but fortunately it is only a small minority of the profession whose doctor/patient relationship ever deteriorates to the point of the patient taking a swing, literally or metaphorically, at his medical adviser.

Two doctors who were concerned in the treatment of a mentally ill patient met in consultation at the patient's house, in order to discuss the advisability of his admission to hospital, but met with great hostility from the patient's wife and family.

Some months later the difficulties of this encounter resulted in a complaint being made about the conduct of the practitioner on whose list the patient was. At the ensuing Service Committee enquiry the respondent practitioner was found blameless and the Chairman remarked that the case should never have been brought.

The failure of the complaint enraged both husband and wife, who then embarked on a campaign of persecution and vilification of the two doctors which involved accosting them on their rounds, sending abusive letters, and causing damage to their property. Unfortunately, no adequate proof was forthcoming of the identity of those responsible for such incidents as the breaking of surgery windows, hence it was not possible to advise legal proceedings. Eventually, however, the occasion presented itself when one of the doctors, on leaving a house on his rounds, had a bucket of earth thrown over him and his car by the aggrieved female complainant. The police were informed, a Summons issued and the prosecution taken over by the doctor's protection society. At the Magistrate's Court the case against the defendant was proved without difficulty and resulted in her being bound over to keep the peace. More important, however, was the fact that she was sufficiently chastened after the hearing to publish in the local paper an apology for her stupid behaviour.

A casualty officer was called one night to attend to a patient who had hurt her hand, and was carrying out his examination when he was interrupted by the patient's companion who was very much the worse for drink. The companion complained that the doctor was hurting the patient. An explanation did not succeed in quietening him and after an altercation the patient's companion seized the doctor by the lapels of his coat, knocked him to the floor and dragged him across the room. The police were summoned, but as they did not see fit to prosecute, for some reason best known to themselves, a private prosecution was undertaken. The defendant pleaded 'not guilty' and asserted that the doctor had threatened him with the words, 'I will get a knife to you and cut your throat with it'. The patient was called as a witness and supported the defendant's allegation, although without much conviction and it was obvious that she had been briefed as to what she should say. The allegation was, of course, too absurd to be taken seriously and can have done the defendant's case no good whatever. The charge was found proved and the Magistrate, describing the defendant's conduct as 'outrageous', gave him a conditional discharge on payment of costs, warning him that any repetition would likely lead to a prison sentence. The conditional discharge was presumably thought more appropriate than a fine, as it would permit this offence to be taken into consideration in the event of the defendant being convicted of a further offence.

Certification

Every year a few doctors find themselves in Court as a result of giving certificates without seeing the patient. The usual story is that the patient's wife attended the surgery saying that her husband was ill again with his old trouble, he had some tablets left over from last time and did not really require a visit, she knew the doctor was very busy but could she have a certificate? The doctor provides the certificate, and although perhaps somewhat surprised that the next week it is again the wife and not the patient who attends, he once again accepts the proffered story and indeed, in some cases, has continued to do so for a matter of months. Sooner or later, however, the doctor receives a visit or a communication from the Department of Health and Social Security and it then appears that his patient has, throughout the period for which he has been issuing certificates, been in prison, or abroad or, quite simply, continuing at his daily work. There is little that can be said in the doctor's defence. A DHSS certificate is, as it were, a cheque on the State and he has signed to the effect that he has examined the patient, knowing full well that such statement is untrue. His conviction is certain, but the more serious aspect of the matter is, of course, the fact that the conviction will be reported to the General Medical Council before whose Professional Conduct Committee he may subsequently have to appear. Even this does not end the troubles which may ensue, for the Ministry may refer the matter to the Local Medical Committee for consideration of whether the doctor has exercised reasonable care in the issuing of certificates, and where, as is almost inevitable, it is found that he has not, a financial penalty may be imposed.

It is perhaps superfluous to add that the one and only protection open to the doctor is to refuse to issue a certificate without seeing the patient. 'Seeing' as opposed to 'examining' is, in general, considered to be adequate, for the word 'examining' is nowhere defined, and visual examination together with, perhaps, interrogation is all that may be required to determine the question of a patient's continued unfitness for work.

Criminal Negligence

It is unlikely in the extreme that any reader will at any time find himself faced with a charge of 'criminal' as opposed to 'civil' negligence, and this heading is included mainly to define criminal negligence and to distinguish it from its much more common civil counterpart.

Criminal negligence then consists of such complete recklessness or disregard for a person to whom one owes a duty of care, as amounts to an offence against the State punishable in the criminal courts. The charge will, according to the circumstances, be one of manslaughter, grievous bodily harm, etc., criminal negligence not itself being a specific offence. The punishment will be in proportion to the negligence. Allegations of criminal negligence against doctors are very uncommon and one has to go back many years to find examples. In 1925, in Rex *v* Bateman, a doctor failed to realise that he had a complete inversion on his hands, and in Rex *v* Wight, another obstetric case, a doctor was sentenced to three months' imprisonment for conducting a forceps delivery while under the influence of chloral hydrate, maternal death resulting.

While there is, in the vast majority of cases, ample excuse where civil negligence is concerned, there can be little in cases of criminal negligence and such matters need, perhaps, concern us no further.

Drinking and Driving

A doctor is at particular risk regarding drinking and driving, in as much as he may be called to an emergency even though he is off duty, and perforce have to drive when he had no intention of so doing.

The Road Traffic Act 1972 makes it an offence to drive, attempt to drive, or be in charge of a motor vehicle on a road or other public place with a blood alcohol exceeding 80 mg/100 ml. Conviction of driving or attempting to drive with a blood alcohol concentration above the prescribed limit, and also conviction of failure to provide a specimen without reasonable excuse is treated as an offence involving obligatory disqualification. In cases of conviction of being in charge of a vehicle with a blood alcohol above the prescribed maximum, or of other offences under the Act, disqualification is discretionary.

The Court is empowered to accept that a 'special reason' exists for not ordering disqualification. A medical emergency could constitute such and, doubtless, would be held to do so were a doctor driving to an emergency while off duty. The reason must be special to the facts of the particular case, not to the individual charged—to the offence not to the offender. The need to drive for business purposes and driving a sick girl home have been held not to amount to 'special reasons'. On the other hand, blood alcohol levels of 82 and 96 mg/100 ml have in the past been accepted as 'special reasons', although in a case in which the level was 85 mg/100 ml the plea of 'special reasons' was rejected, and it is perhaps likely that the latter view will be followed in the future.

Drugs and Drug Legislation

Drug legislation becomes increasingly complex as drugs themselves become more complex and abuse of drugs becomes more common. The practising doctor has comparatively few rules to obey because of the numerous exemptions which apply to him throughout the legislation. It cannot however be too strongly stressed that all these exemptions attach not to the doctor by virtue of his possessing a medical qualification, but to his needs in giving adequate care to his patients. A doctor who deals in drugs in any manner other than the care of his patients is in precisely the same position as any other individual dealing similarly, and is subject to precisely the same controls. It therefore behoves the doctor to have at least a nodding acquaintance with drugs legislation that he may appreciate the limits of his rights, and also his essential duties so far as drugs are concerned.

Medicines Acts 1968 and 1971

The purpose of the Medicines Acts was to enable the Government to exert statutory control over virtually every aspect of drug handling. Under the Acts, regulations have been and will be made regarding the manufacture, testing, marketing, importing, exporting and selling of all types of medicinal products.

To enable the responsible Ministers to carry out these duties, the 1968 Act set up the Medicines Commission to give advice generally or as requested. The professions concerned are represented on the Commission. Also established under the Act were the Committee on Safety of Medicines, and the British Pharmacopoeial Commission.

Orders made under the Act have classified medicinal products into three lists: a general sales list, a pharmacy sales list, and a prescription only medicines list. By the Medicines (Prescriptions Only) Order 1980, doctors, dentists and veterinary practitioners are alone authorised to prescribe medicines on the Prescriptions Only List. There are inevitably certain medicines exempted from the order by virtue of their being below a prescribed strength, or because of the method of their administration, e.g. when used for external application.

The order requires doctors, when prescribing a medicine on the Prescriptions Only List, to sign it in ink, to write the prescription in ink unless it is an NHS one not for a controlled drug, in which case it may be by means of carbon paper or similar material. The prescription must contain the doctor's address, the date and the name, address and, if under twelve, the age of the patient.

A pharmacist is permitted to supply in emergency where a doctor, unable to give an immediate prescription, has undertaken to do so within 72 hours. Where a controlled drug is sought (see page 97) the pharmacist is required to interview the person seeking the drug and to satisfy himself of the immediate need for it.

The Secretary of State, or in effect the DHSS, is the licensing authority for the various licences and certificates required by manufacturers, wholesalers, etc. The one which particularly concerns doctors is the clinical trial certificate, and doctors taking part in clinical trials should satisfy themselves that the certificate has been obtained and that the trial is being conducted as required by the terms of the certificate.

It bears repeating that the exemptions granted to doctors relate solely to their use of medicinal products for the treatment of their patients. Where a doctor imports, or has imported, manufactures, or has manufactured, a medicinal product for a particular patient, neither licence nor certificate is required. Should he wish to deal with medicinal products in circumstances other than the care of his patients he should first make himself *au fait* with the up-to-date licensing requirements.

Misuse of Drugs Act 1971

This Act codified previous legislation regarding dangerous drugs and their misuse. At the same time it and the regulations made under it extended the powers of Government in many aspects of drug control and imposed a series of penalties for contravention.

The drugs controlled by the Act are, in the Misuse of Drugs Regulations 1973, divided into four schedules. Schedule I exempts certain preparations of Schedule II drugs from the regulations applicable to drugs in Schedule II, by virtue of the low concentration of the drug in the particular preparation.

Schedule II is the most important schedule so far as the practising doctor is concerned. In it are the narcotics, heroin, morphine and various derivatives, and preparations of opium, cocaine, pethidine, and the amphetamines.

Schedule III is of little practical importance, listing as it does at present a mere handful of drugs, none of which are extensively used in practice.

Schedule IV contains drugs which have little use in medicine, but are extensively misused in other quarters. Cannabis, LSD, raw opium and various other hallucinogens appear here, and any dealing in Schedule IV drugs, be it production, possession, supply or administration, requires licensing by the Home Office.

Doctors in the conduct of their medical practices are authorised to manufacture, possess, supply, administer and cause to be administered by another person, drugs in Schedules II and III. Limited authority is given to matrons of hospitals and nursing homes, where there is no pharmacist. A ward or theatre sister may only supply such a drug to a patient in the ward or theatre when acting on the instructions of a doctor or dentist. Midwives may possess and administer pethidine in the practice of their profession.

Prescriptions for controlled drugs in Schedules II or III must be in ink, signed and dated by the doctor. The patient's name and address must be in the doctor's own handwriting, as must the dose, the form

Part I

Entries to be made in case of obtaining

Date on which supply received	Name	Address	Amount obtained	Form in which obtained
	Of person or firm from whom obtained			

Part II

Entries to be made in case of supply

Date on which the transaction was effected	Name	Address	Particulars as to licence or authority of person or firm supplied to be in possession	Amount supplied	Form in which supplied
	Of person or firm supplied				

of preparation—tablets, capsules etc.,—and, where appropriate, the strength of the preparation. Either the total quantity to be dispensed or the number of doses must be written both in figures and words. Should the total quantity be ordered to be dispensed in instalments then the amount and number of instalments and the intervals between their being dispensed must also be stated.

The pharmacist may not dispense a prescription for a controlled drug in Schedules II and III unless it conforms with the requirements, the address of the practitioner is in the UK, and either the dispenser is acquainted with the signature of the prescriber, or has taken reasonable steps to assure himself that the prescription is genuine. The prescription may not be dispensed later than 13 weeks after the date which appears on it.

Hospital prescribing on treatment sheets or on case notes is regarded as an instruction to the sister in charge to supply from ward stocks, and the handwriting requirements do not apply. Should the controlled drug require to be obtained from the dispensary then the requirements should be complied with.

Where a doctor wishes to obtain drugs controlled by Schedules II and III for use in his practice, the requisition must be written and signed by him, give his name, address, and occupation, state the purpose for which the drugs are to be used and the amount required. Again the pharmacist must satisfy himself that the requisition is genuine. Emergency supplies can be obtained in the absence of a written requisition by the doctor undertaking to supply one within 24 hours.

Drugs Registers must be kept for Schedule II and IV drugs. Any bound—not loose-leaf—book can be used, and the entries in chronological order should be shown, as in the diagram on page 98.

A separate section should be used for each class of drug, and entries must be made on the day the drug is obtained or supplied, or should this not be practicable, on the day following. Alterations must be made by dated marginal entries, not by cancellation or by obliteration. Entries must be in ink, separate Registers kept for separate premises, and the Register must be available for inspection by authorised inspectors from the Home Office or DHSS. Registers must be retained for two years after the last entry.

There is of course no need to record prescriptions for controlled drugs given to patients for dispensing by a pharmacist.

Disposal of Controlled Drugs

It was in the past common practice for general practitioners to collect dangerous drugs remaining where a patient had died or no longer required them, and to use them as necessary for other patients. Since the 1971 Act required a record to be made of drugs administered, other than when obtained on a patient's prescription, such a procedure could lead a doctor into difficulties. In any event such drugs are the property of the patient, and the correct procedure is for doctors to advise patients or relatives to destroy them—burning them or flushing them down the toilet may be appropriate.

Where a doctor has obtained controlled drugs and later does not wish to retain them, he should have them destroyed in the presence of an authorised person, the most convenient such person being a police officer. The authorised person should sign the entry regarding the quantity destroyed.

Misuse of Drugs (Safe Custody) Regulations 1973

These Regulations require controlled drugs, with certain exemptions, to be kept in a locked receptacle, access to which is available only to the practitioner or other authorised person. The case of Kemeswara Rao *v* Wyles* went to appeal and resulted in a Court decision to the effect that a locked car was not a 'locked receptacle' within the meaning of the Act. The most a doctor can do, if he is to carry controlled drugs at all, is to keep them in a locked bag in a locked car. If then the locked car is not a 'locked receptacle' it follows that the locked bag must be so considered. In this event no offence would appear to be committed if the car is left unlocked, or indeed with the doors wide open, provided that the bag itself is locked. Where, however, drugs are stolen from a car which a doctor fails to lock, the doctor will inevitably come in for criticism from any Court before which the facts of the matter may subsequently be related, so it would seem that in this instance the law wants it both ways and, meanwhile, doctors suffer from a decision which offends against common sense.

Misuse of Drugs (Notification of Supply to Addicts) Regulations 1973

An addict is considered to be a person who has, as a result of repeated

* (1949) 2 All ER 685.

administration, become so dependent upon a drug that he has an overpowering desire for the administration of it to be continued.

The Regulations require doctors to notify the Chief Medical Officer at the Home Office in writing within seven days of the name, address, sex, date of birth, NHS number, so far as these particulars may be known to him, together with the date of attendance and the drug or drugs involved when a patient is considered to be addicted to any of the listed drugs. This list, which may be varied from time to time, contains at present the following drugs:

Cocaine
Dextromoradmide (Palfium)
Dipipanone (Diconal, Pipadone*)
Hydrocodone (Dicodid)
Hydromorphone (Dilaudid)
Levorphanol (Dromoran)
Oxycodone (Proladone)
Pethidine (Pamergan, Pethilorfan)
Methadone (Physeptone)
Morphine (Cyclimorph, Duromorph*, Mortha*)
Opium
Papaveretum (Omnopon)†
Phenazocine (Narphen)
Piritramide (Dipidolor)

No notification is necessary where the doctor considers the administration of the drug necessary for the treatment of organic disease, nor if notification has been made by a colleague in the practice or hospital within the preceding twelve months.

No doctor other than one specially licensed may administer or supply heroin or cocaine, except in the treatment of organic disease or injury, to any person addicted to any of the listed drugs.

Administration of the Act

The Act brought into being the Advisory Council on the Misuse of Drugs, charged with keeping the situation regarding misuse under review, and of advising the Ministers of measures which they feel should be taken to prevent misuse, and to remedy its effects.

Where the Secretary of State considers that there exists a social problem regarding the misuse of drugs he may require doctors and pharmacists in that area to give details of drugs prescribed or supplied. A pharmacist may be required to give the names of doctors

*Manufacture of these drugs has been discontinued but there may be residual stocks in some places.

†Papaveretum (Omnopon) contains other opium alkaloids but is controlled because of its morphine content.

who have prescribed controlled drugs, but neither doctor nor pharmacist may be required to give the names of the patients involved.

The second schedule to the Act—as opposed to Schedule II of the 1973 Regulations referred to on page 97—divides controlled drugs into three lists, A, B and C, with relation to the penalties incurred for various offences under the Act, on the principle that offences relating to the more addictive drugs attract higher penalties.

The offences to which doctors are particularly liable include, failing to keep controlled drugs in a locked receptacle accessible only to those authorised to possess controlled drugs, failure to keep Registers, or to produce them to an authorised person, failure to notify addicts, or prescribing heroin or cocaine without being licensed so to do. The penalties for such offences in the case of a Class A drug range up to 14 years' imprisonment.

Following conviction of an offence under the Act or under the Customs and Excise Act 1952 relating to the importing or exporting of controlled drugs, the Secretary of State may remove from a doctor his authority to possess, prescribe, administer, manufacture, or supply controlled drugs.

Where a doctor has been found by a tribunal to have offended against the Notification of and Supply to Addicts Regulations, he may be prohibited from prescribing, administering or supplying controlled drugs.

Irresponsible prescribing may also lead to a doctor's authority to prescribe, administer or supply being withdrawn. He will usually in the first place have been advised by an inspector from the Home Office, but should such advice be ignored, or the irresponsible prescribing be gross, the matter is referred to a tribunal for consideration. Should the tribunal advise that the Secretary of State should make a direction removing a doctor's authority in respect of certain drugs, the doctor may make representations which will be considered by an advisory body, following which the final decision will be made.

Poisons Act 1972

Under this Act a distinction is made between substances used in medical, dental and veterinary practice and those used for domestic purposes. Pharmacists only may dispense substances in the former list, and then only on a practitioner's prescription. Prescriptions for drugs listed must be in writing, give name and address of patient and of practitioner, total quantity, and authorise repetition of dispensing.

Apart from drugs also controlled by the Misuse of Drugs Act, the main drugs involved under the Poisons Act are the barbiturates.

So much for the legislation, but law is not everything. Doctors may all too easily become addicted to drugs and this can lead not only to penalties under the law, but to an appearance before the GMC. The law permits a doctor to prescribe controlled drugs for himself, but common sense surely dictates otherwise. Patients going abroad may seek prescriptions of controlled drugs, and the prudent doctor will, except in the case of short stays abroad, prescribe such amount as he considers to be necessary until his patient can reasonably consult a doctor overseas.

The responsibility is on the doctor to maintain a reasonable degree of suspicion of new patients seeking controlled drugs, for much abuse is made possible by over-prescribing, carelessness with prescription pads, and sheer gullibility.

There exists a type of person who makes it his business to call when a new casualty officer is appointed, or when the general practitioner is on holiday and a locum is standing in. He appears with, perhaps, a story of having just arrived in the district from the far end of the country to see a dying relative and having forgotten his tablets. He may suggest that he has been diagnosed as having narcolepsy at a famous hospital a very long way away, and states that he was told that he must never be without his tablets and produces a grubby amphetamine tablet wrapped up in a handkerchief; or, alternatively, he was suicidal, just rescued in the nick of time, and although many doctors have tried to change him from whatever he was taking to something else, they have always had to put him back on to it; he dare not be without it; he does not know what he might do to himself. The stories are legion but the medical cards are never presented, the telephone number of the doctor or hospital who prescribed the drug is never known, and an offer to help on receipt of a note from the doctor or hospital is never followed up. A report of the matter giving a description of the patient—for the name and address will almost inevitably prove to be false—to the Family Practitioner Committee may help to prevent other doctors being deceived.

Doctors are sometimes worried about reporting these people, having regard to professional confidence. A moment's thought, however, will show that these are not *bona fide* patients but con men, to whom the doctor owes no duty of confidentiality.

Doctors have from time to time been criticised regarding National Health Service prescription forms, and while not every critic appears to be very well informed, nevertheless there is a clear duty on practitioners to exercise care in the use of these forms. Some while ago the writer called into his local chemist's and found the chemist's wife, who assisted in the shop, panting heavily, yet giving also the impression that her excessive respiratory excursion was actuated by exasperation as well as by exertion. It appeared, upon enquiry, that returning from her lunch she had observed an F.P.10 being blown with some rapidity down the street past the chemist's shop. Being well aware of the need for care in the distribution of F.P.10's, she, a somewhat rotund and matronly figure, had pursued the errant form and in due course had overtaken and captured her prize. The four words written thereon did nothing to restore her respiratory equipoise. They read 'TWO PINTS TODAY PLEASE'.

Forms being left out for collection by patients, parts of the form being left blank, the almost universal use of the ball point pen, numbers being written so that a '1' can easily be put in front of them, all combine to make the task of the habitual drug taker and the pedlar far from arduous.

Chemists' Obligations *re* Prescriptions

Doctors are sometimes very put out when they find that a chemist declines to dispense a controlled drug or scheduled poison at their request. In the first place, it should be realised that chemists, like other shopkeepers, are under no obligation to sell that which they have in their shop. Even a price tag on an article displayed in a shop is not an offer to sell at that price, but merely an invitation to treat. Secondly, the chemist is required to satisfy himself that a prescription is written by a registered practitioner, and it is for him to decide what evidence he requires before he is so satisfied. The fact that a person can give a name in the Medical Register and show a driving licence with a doctor's name is hardly conclusive evidence of identity. Such difficulties usually arise where junior hospital doctors require a prescription for themselves or for a member of their family. If the patient is not being treated as a hospital patient, the hospital dispensary cannot properly be used and so recourse is made to the chemist, and the doctor tends to feel that he has a right to have his prescription dispensed. An introduction to the chemist by another doctor or through the hospital pharmacist should avoid all difficulty.

7 Civil Law

Only three matters of civil law have relevance to the doctor as a practitioner, namely assault, defamation, and negligence. While the last of these, negligence, can perhaps only operate in one direction—it is difficult to imagine circumstances in which the doctor could allege negligence against his patient—in cases of assault or defamation he may find himself in the position of plaintiff or defendant.

Assault

By the Doctor

Perhaps any medical examination other than the purely visual could constitute an assault at law, if the patient or someone acting for him had not consented to the procedure. It follows then that the basis of an action in assault against a doctor is an allegation of lack of consent.

Consent, to be valid, must be 'real'; that is to say, the patient must understand to what he is asked to consent. This does not mean that he must be told of every possible complication which could occur, nor that he must be told the obvious. The law only requires that he be given information suitable to his education and intelligence to permit him to assess fairly the proposed examination or treatment. In one case, it was alleged against a surgeon that the risk of haemorrhage during an operation had not been mentioned when consent was requested. This contention was rejected by the Court with the observation that such a risk was common knowledge which did not require specific reference. On the other hand, there is little doubt that, if a surgeon decided in the course of an operation for simple fibroids to perform a hysterectomy on a woman prior to the menopause without mentioning this possibility and obtaining her consent, an action in assault would lie.

In consequence, the practice still in use in some hospitals of having consent forms for 'whatever may be necessary' signed by the patient on admission is of very little value. The patient in many cases cannot be properly aware of what he is consenting to and such consent has no validity.

Consent may be written, oral, or implied. All are of equal merit in law, though written consent has the advantage of providing a permanent record. But written consent for every minor procedure would clearly be impractical. The patient who presents with a superficial abscess and who cooperates in the preparation for its incision cannot later allege assault because he was not asked to sign a consent form. Few hard and fast rules can be given regarding the circumstances which make written consent necessary. It is certainly advisable in all cases where general anaesthetics are to be given, for the great majority of surgical procedures, for ECT, and in procedures, other than the most trivial, involving children or persons detained in mental hospitals or under guardianship orders.

The question of consent can give rise to difficulties in a number of circumstances. Age seldom causes much difficulty since the Family Law Reform Act of 1969, which stated that a person of 16 could give valid consent. The Act left open the question of whether, and if so in what circumstances, a person under the age of 16 could consent.

Common sense must rule here, and it would be as unreasonable to refuse to insert a suture under local anaesthetic for a 15-year-old's cut finger, when he has arrived with a note from his mother saying that she wonders whether the cut needs stitching, as it would be to carry out a major non-urgent procedure on a patient of the same age without seeking parental consent.

Whenever a doctor is faced with a person urgently requiring treatment and no valid consent is available, whether because the patient is unconscious, mentally incapable, a child, or for other reasons, he cannot be thought at any appreciable risk if he gives whatever treatment is immediately necessary. If an action were brought the doctor could claim to have been an agent of necessity, acting in what he had reason to believe would be the manner in which the patient or those responsible for him would desire. The slight risk from such an action must be accepted. To delay treatment while seeking consent would be to act contrary to the patient's interests, and would also risk an action in negligence should damage flow from the delay. Treatment in such circumstances should, however, be limited to that immediately necessary to save life or prevent serious harm resulting. To extend treatment to include anything which could await consent would be, in today's climate, to risk being found guilty of assault, battery, or trespass to the person.

It is more difficult when parents unreasonably withhold consent for treatment thought essential to a child's welfare. This is perhaps most likely when parents, for religious reasons, withhold permission for a blood transfusion. It is reasonable to tell such parents that their views will be respected as far as is compatible with the child's welfare, but it should be made clear that an essential transfusion will be given. The parents may state their intention of removing the child from hospital. When such is the case they should be told quite clearly that they will be jeopardising the child's life and that, should the child die, the coroner will be informed. The author is unaware of any legal difficulty arising for a doctor when this has been done. It appears to deter parents from removing a child and when the transfusion has been given nothing more has been said. If parents take the child from medical care having been informed that it might well die as a result, they would, having regard to the decision in Regina *v* Senior* and the Judge's remarks in Regina *v* Spencer and Spencer†, put themselves in danger of a charge of manslaughter. Having regard to the House of Lords decision in the cases of Regina *v* J. H. Sheppard, and Regina *v* J. C. Sheppard‡, it is essential that a record should be made of the advice given, as an offence of wilful neglect under the Children and Young Persons Act 1933 requires it to be shown that the parent or custodian of the child was aware of the need for medical attention, or alternatively that his unawareness was due to his not caring whether or not the child's health was at risk. For the doctor to transfuse, and thereby save the child, cannot be thought to place him at any appreciable risk; nor would it do so were the child to die, provided there had been no negligence. Some hospital authorities have taken the step of having the child removed from the parents' care and placed under the care of the local authority. They have then obtained consent from an officer of that authority. Apart from the time involved, this is an unnecessarily complex method of dealing with a generally straightforward problem.

Persons whose mental state precludes their giving a valid consent present a common difficulty. Such people may or may not be in-patients in mental hospitals, and if so, may or may not be informal patients. Only when patients are under legal guardianship is there any certainty as to who should give consent. For the rest, the patient himself, even though detained in hospital, the nearest relative or the

* (1899) 1 QB 283. † *The Times*, 1 March 1953.
‡ *The Times*, 2 December 1980.

responsible medical officer may be appropriate, depending on the urgency of the treatment required and the understanding of the patient. The most serious difficulty arises when a patient, compulsorily detained in hospital under the Mental Health Act, appears to appreciate the reasons for the treatment advised but declines to give consent. The doctor may feel that he knows where the patient's interests lie, and may be tempted to circumvent the problem by obtaining the consent of the responsible medical officer. However, it can hardly be thought proper to deprive a person of his right to decline consent solely because he happens to be detained under the Mental Health Act.

On occasion, it may be wise to seek the consent of the nearest relative. In cases of accident or serious illness the patient may not be able to give consent, and while urgently needed treatment must not be delayed, if a relative is available it is a useful safeguard to obtain his signature on the consent form. Difficulties may however arise if the relative refuses to sign. His refusal may be based on his, the relative's, religious convictions and here there can be no doubt that the doctor should act as an agent of necessity and carry out the required treatment. But the relative may refuse consent saying he believes the proposed treatment would be against the wishes of the patient. Here one cannot speak with authority, but the view is expressed that where it is uncertain whether the patient, appreciating the full consequences of refusal, would still withhold consent, the doctor should act in the way be believes to be in the patient's best interests irrespective of the relative's views.

At the time of writing there is considerable doubt regarding patients admitted under Section 26 of the Mental Health Act, that is, admitted under a treatment order. On the one hand it is argued that it would be absurd for Parliament to institute treatment orders if the patient could refuse all treatment. The other view is that had Parliament intended to remove the individual's right to accept or refuse treatment from any specified group of people it would have done so in express terms. The Act is at present under review and it is to be hoped that this area of doubt will be clarified.

Procedures which affect a patient's reproductive capacity or ability to participate in sexual intercourse sometimes give rise to doubt. Essentially such procedures do not differ from those on other parts of the body. The adult patient, male or female, married or single, is competent to consent to the proposed procedure, and seeking the consent of the spouse is a courtesy and not a legal requirement. It is of course essential that the patient should understand the effect of the procedure on his or her sexual functions, for this is clearly an aspect to be taken into account in giving or withholding consent.

Should the procedure be recommended for sound medical reasons, then clearly the doctor cannot allow the spouse's objection to influence the treatment he considers necessary and his patient wishes to receive. Should the procedure be one of convenience only, e.g. the fitting of an intra-uterine contraceptive device or a sterilisation for birth control purposes without medical need, then, whilst the doctor is legally entitled to accept the consent of the patient, it is for him to determine whether he wishes to carry out such procedures in the absence of joint consent of both parties.

Consent for Clinical Trials

It has already been indicated that for consent to be valid the patient must be told all that he reasonably needs to know and wishes to hear about the proposed procedure to enable him to make a reasonable decision. It is in clinical trials that the greatest care must be taken to ensure that the patient is adequately informed. Doctors concerned in such trials are at special risk of allegations being made against them. It is preferable if an entirely independent doctor assures himself that the subjects appreciate the nature of the trial, such risks as are known, the possibility of unknown risks, and also that the consent is freely given without there being any duress on the one hand or feeling of obligation on the other. Whilst the single standard consent form is adequate for all therapeutic and investigative procedures, a special form drawn up with regard to the particular circumstances is recommended for subjects of clinical trials.

Consent for Post Mortems

No consent is required where the coroner orders a post mortem examination.

In other circumstances the Human Tissue Act 1961 requires that 'the person lawfully in possession of the body' authorises both post mortem examination and removal of tissue. The person lawfully in possession is the hospital authority until such time as a relative claims possession. In the absence of a signed consent by the deceased, e.g. a kidney donor card, the hospital authority or relative as the case may be must, following such enquiry as may be practicable, satisfy himself that there is no reason to believe that the deceased would have objected, or that another relative objects to the proposed examination or removal of tissue. A form on which the relative can declare his lack of objection is provided by the DHSS.

Cases on Consent

Cases are few and older ones may no longer reflect the attitude of the Court today. There is a trend, when a patient has suffered a complication, towards alleging either that as the specific complication had not been mentioned, then the consent was invalid and the procedure therefore an assault, or alternatively that the doctor was negligent in failing to mention the complication.

In re D (a minor) 1976*, the Court upheld an objection raised by a third party to a proposed sterilisation of an 11-year-old girl with Soto's Syndrome. The child's mother was in favour of the sterilisation and this case illustrates the limitation of a parent's right to consent to a non-therapeutic procedure which the Court considers not to be medically necessary, nor in the best interests of the child.

The lack of any legal right held by a putative father to object to an abortion being carried out, was made clear in Paton *v* Trustees of British Pregnancy Advisory Services 1978†. The patient's consent is the only legal requirement, but as pointed out in the section on abortion, there are cases where the doctor will wish to take the father's opinion into consideration in determining the legality or otherwise of the procedure in a particular case.

In Chatterton *v* Gerson and Another‡, the plaintiff alleged assault against a doctor on the grounds that he had failed adequately to advise her of the effects of an intrathecal block for intractible pain. The injection was the second the patient had had for the same purpose and the Court held that there was no need for the explanation of the effects of the procedure to be spelt out a second time. In an important distinction between action in trespass, i.e. assault, and in negligence, the Court said that once the patient was informed in broad terms of the nature of the procedure and gave her consent, that consent was real, i.e. no action in trespass would lie. A claim based

* (1976) Fam. 185 (1976) 1 All ER 326.

† (1978) 2 All ER 987. ‡ *The Times*, 7 February 1980.

on failure to go into the risks and implications of a procedure was based in negligence not in trespass.

Too often, unfortunately, an allegation of lack of consent is based or irrefutable fact and settlement is the only course.

A patient was admitted to hospital, the notes and the letter to the GP showing clearly that the intention was to carry out a Manchester repair. The day before the operation the surgeon decided to perform a vaginal hysterectomy, told a nurse of his intention, and she proceeded to alter the entry on the consent form from 'Repair' to 'Vaginal hysterectomy'. No one, it appeared, thought to discuss the matter with the patient, though it must be mentioned that as the patient's age was approaching the half century, some might have thought that the retention of her uterus was not a matter of great moment. An assault had, however, been committed, the patient lost no time in making her claim, and the only problem was agreeing the amount to be paid in settlement. As so often in such cases, the patient put an absurd value on her uterus, stating that she had intended to have at least two more children—her youngest child was approaching his teens—but no defence to the claim itself was possible.

Assault may also be alleged if the patient has reason to consider that a particular surgeon has contracted to operate and the operation is conducted by some other person. For this reason, it is important that the consent form should make it clear that no such promise has been made. Mitchell *v* Molesworth* was a case in which a house surgeon successfully carried out a herniorrhaphy, but the patient succeeded in his action against the consultant on the rather strange basis that his house surgeon had operated without consent. The Judge, finding no breach of contract against the surgeon but a technical trespass, awarded twenty shillings without costs, allowing the surgeon his counterclaim for three guineas consultation fee plus the costs of the counterclaim. He added that the action ought not to have been brought.

Since this case, consent forms usually contain a sentence to the effect that the patient appreciates that no promise is given that the operation will be carried out by a particular surgeon. However, difficulty has recurred in the case of private patients by whom, traditionally but unfortunately, consent forms are usually not signed. In private cases, if there is to be a change of surgeon, even though it is

* *Brit. Med. J.*, 15 July 1950, 171: *Lancet*, 24 June 1950, 1168.

for the very best of reasons, all concerned are at risk unless the patient is informed of the proposed change and consent obtained.

Assault on Doctor

Unfortunately, cases of doctors being assaulted by their patient are not exceedingly rare, and each year a few such cases come to the notice of the Medical Protection Society. Where, as is usual, no serious damage has been suffered, it is appropriate to have the offender dealt with in the criminal court, and two such cases are reported in the chapter on Criminal Law. When the contrary is the case civil proceedings may additionally or alternatively be undertaken. The decision as to appropriate action in any case is one on which the doctor should take advice. Knowledge of how the local bench views private prosecutions, the reputation of the County Court, and other matters unlikely to be within the knowledge of the doctor, may be helpful.

A casualty officer was called at night to examine an extremely inebriated patient. He complained of pain in the chest and the doctor's efforts at auscultation were rendered valueless by the constant shouting and swearing of the patient. Eventually the doctor, in somewhat strident tones and possibly abrupt terms, extolled the virtues of silence and, for his pains, was rewarded with a full blooded punch on the nose which caused a minor fracture. The patient was facing a police prosecution in respect of driving in his besotted condition, the local Magistrates were reported as not favouring private prosecutions, clear damage with X-ray evidence had been suffered, so the doctor was advised that a civil action in the County Court was indicated and this was successfully undertaken.

Defamation

Defamation may be defined as a false statement about a man to his discredit, or which exposes him to hatred, ridicule, or contempt. The test as applied by Lord Aitken was, 'Would the words tend to lower the plaintiff in the estimation of right thinking members of society generally?' It amounts to libel when the statement is in permanent form, i.e. writing, printing, carving, or broadcasting, and slander where the words were conveyed in some form which is not lasting, i.e. speech or gesture. In general, an action in libel requires no proof of loss, libel being actionable *per se*. Slander requires proof of actual loss with certain exceptions, the only one relevant here being when the slander is calculated to disparage the plaintiff in respect of his profession or trade.

Defence to a charge of defamation may be based on the substantial truth of the words, fair comment on a matter of public interest, apology and offer of amends, or privilege. So far as doctors are concerned there is no absolute privilege. Qualified privilege may be claimed where the words complained of were conveyed to a third party who had an interest in the matter, and the doctor either had a legal duty to inform the third party or, alternatively, a moral or ethical obligation so to do. A defence of qualified privilege will not succeed if the patient can show that the defendant doctor was actuated by malice. In its legal sense, malice may be interpreted as embracing any motivation of an improper nature.

The essence of defamation is that there has been a publication to a third party which is not covered by privilege, and this fact immediately disposes of the desire of many doctors to institute legal proceedings because of something some patient has written to a hospital, Family Practitioner Committee, or to themselves.

Before considering doctors defamed, however, a thought about defaming doctors.

Defamation by a Doctor

'Mr X tells me he has been my HS for six months and you will be lucky if you get him to work for you', is probably sufficiently double-edged to avoid being defamatory, but giving testimonials is one way in which doctors are liable to become involved in defamation issues. Testimonials can certainly claim qualified privilege, but if a reasonable testimonial cannot be given it is better to refuse one altogether. A false testimonial may itself be actionable, and one which damns with faint praise is of no use to anyone. If, however, one honestly and without malice makes a statement to persons having a legitimate interest in receiving it, then though the statement be false no action for defamation will lie.

Just how complicated libel actions may become is shown by the following case.

An action for damages was brought by a motorist against the owners and driver of a car with which he had been in collision. Liability had been admitted but the claim was so substantial that the insurers determined to contest the quantum of damages in Court. The Judge awarded the plaintiff a very substantial sum, but stated his opinion that the plaintiff had been more interested in the question of compensation than in making a real effort to get well after the accident.

Before these proceedings came to Court the plaintiff had embarked on other proceedings alleging that libellous remarks had been published about him in a medical report which had been submitted to the insurers. The doctor concerned had examined the plaintiff at the request of the insurers' solicitors and had stated that, at the time of his examination, the patient's disabilities were no longer serious and were largely of a functional nature. He quoted certain conversations with the patient and referred to his demeanour as almost a caricature . . . the patient lying in bed smoking a cigar, the picture of comfort, cock-sure, arrogant, and self-opinionated. For some reason the insurers' solicitors saw fit to quote some parts of the medical report to the patient's solicitors including this adverse reference. The Medical Protection Society acted for the doctor, and their solicitors in due course issued a Summons to strike out the Statement of Claim on the grounds that it disclosed no reasonable cause of action. This contention was accepted, the action dismissed with costs, but the plaintiff promptly appealed to a Judge in Chambers who allowed the appeal on the ground that the doctor's report enjoyed only qualified privilege. Leave to appeal against this decision was refused by the Judge and later refused again by the Court of Appeal. The plaintiff's solicitors then proceeded with the libel action, but a further dispute arose in connection with the discovery of relevant documents. In legal proceedings it is usual for the parties to furnish a list stating what documents, other than those covered by privilege, have been in their possession and the Society's solicitors did not include in their list the reports supplied by the doctor. The plaintiff's solicitors issued a summons asking that an Order of the Court be made for their production, and when this came before a Master of the High Court the view that the documents were privileged was supported. Once again, however, the decision was reversed by a Judge, and on appeal to the Court of Appeal two Judges found in favour of the plaintiff with the third dissenting. The libel action therefore continued, the plaintiff's solicitors making repeated efforts to induce the Society to make some payment to their client. Finally, before the case came to trial, an application by the plaintiff to discontinue the action was granted by the Court and so the matter ended.

Defamation of a Doctor

Doctors not uncommonly seek to bring actions in defamation in respect of articles in newspapers. What they often fail to realise is that a newspaper has a perfect right to quote them or to insert their photographs without their permission. Whether defamation proceedings are possible depends entirely upon the content of the article.

In the Republic of Ireland a report appeared in a magazine stating that after a recent election it had been said by the loser that certain patients in a mental hospital had been subjected to undue influence by their doctors before voting. This allegation, the truth of which was denied, appeared to be defamatory of the members of the medical staff of the hospital and, as an identifiable body, thus to give each and every one of them a right of action. The publishers were therefore pressed for a full withdrawal and apology together with payment of an appropriate sum by way of compensation. The original offer to publish an apology and to pay reasonable legal costs only was regarded as inadequate and the matter was pursued until both a withdrawal and also a modest sum as an earnest of the published apology were received.

A second case concerned an article in a local newspaper. It referred to a meeting of an executive council, the forerunner of the present Family Practitioner Committee, at which the result of an appeal by a doctor to the Minister against a decision of the executive council was received. The circumstances concerned the doctor's refusal to allow his surgery to be inspected by a sub-committee of the Local Medical Committee. A Medical Service Committee found the doctor in breach of his Terms of Service and recommended that £50 be withheld from his remuneration. The member appealed to the Minister, who upheld the finding but decided to waive the fine, provided the doctor agreed to the proposed inspection. The press report of which the doctor complained was headed 'Ministry Quash Fine' and then in very large type 'Doctor Has Been Put On Probation'. The report itself dealt briefly with the Minister's decision and quoted remarks of certain members of the executive council including the statement, 'he has been put on probation, no fine imposed'. It was considered that the remark of the executive council member, though defamatory, was probably privileged, but that privilege did not extend to the newspaper which had published the report of the proceedings. It was pointed out to the editor that to publish a statement that a person had been put on probation carries with it an implication that the individual has been guilty of some criminal offence and is libellous, and that unless a correction and apology were published forthwith, proceedings would be issued. The newspaper acted promptly and an approved statement appeared in the next issue correcting the false impression.

Negligence

Civil negligence is a 'tort' which consists of a failure to exercise a duty of care resulting in damage. The redress which the Court will award to a successful plaintiff is such sum as is deemed to compensate for the damage suffered. From this it follows that in civil negligence the degree of negligence is immaterial. If a doctor's act of omission is deemed by the Court to have been negligent, and if serious harm results, then no matter how slight the doctor's fault, heavy damages will be awarded. Conversely, gross carelessness which does not lead to any harm will not ground a case in civil law, or to put it another way, it would give the patient a very good claim to nothing.

It is salutary to reflect that a doctor is at risk every time his standard falls below that of competent practitioner of his class and experience. No doctor is long qualified before he appreciates that there are times when, from exhaustion, anxiety, illness, or other cause, he is not cerebrating or communicating with his patient as well as usual. If, from such a lapse, harm should result, a claim in negligence could follow, and this necessarily implies that every practising doctor is at some time at risk.

Risk may be present at every stage of a doctor's contact with his patients, in his diagnosis, his advice, his treatment or his communications with others concerned with the patient's welfare.

The remainder of this chapter, after a brief historical survey, will comprise cases in which doctors have been involved in the early years of their careers. No doubt their experiences will point the moral 'There but for the grace of God . . .' more effectively than could any sermonising.

It was as long ago as 1838, in the case of Lanphier *v* Phipos*, that it was laid down that a person in a learned profession undertook to bring to it reasonable skill and care, and in 1862, in Rich *v* Pierpont†, it was stressed that a doctor was not negligent merely because another practitioner might have shown greater skill. In 1909, in

* 8 C&P 475. † 3 F&F 35.

Hillyer *v* St Bartholomew's Hospital*, it was decided that a hospital authority was not responsible for the negligent acts of its doctors, but this view was opposed in 1951 in Cassidy *v* Ministry of Health† when it was decided that although consultants have a 'contract for services', not a 'contract of service', a hospital authority is, nevertheless, under a duty of care which it is not empowered to delegate. The liability of hospitals was further extended in 1952 when it was determined that a hospital was liable, not only for the negligence of an inexperienced anaesthetist, but also for having entrusted the relevant operation to her (Jones *v* Manchester Corporation‡).

In 1948, in Whiteford *v* Hunter and Gleed§, the finding of the Court of first instance was reversed on appeal. A surgeon was found negligent in failing to use a special cystoscope and in failing to request microscopic examination, but the Court of Appeal determined that there had been no negligence in that the surgeon had followed a course approved by a responsible body of the profession. In 1954, in Roe *v* Ministry of Health¶, a most tragic case in which phenol seeped through invisible cracks in an ampoule of local anaesthetic to be used for spinal anaesthesia, and resulted in permanent paralysis of the lower half of the body, it was stated that one must not condemn as negligent that which is only misadventure. In Bolam *v* Friern HMC‖, where a patient suffered fractures during electro-convulsive therapy given without muscle relaxants and not having been warned of the possible risks, the Court found for the hospital on the grounds, first, that there was a responsible body of medical opinion which approved of the practice and, second, that in so far as the patient was not warned, this again was an approved practice. To succeed, the plaintiff would have had to show that he would have refused treatment had he been warned of the risks.

There must be a direct causative relationship between the act or omission complained of and the harm suffered. A workman suffered a cut leg owing to the negligence of his employers, the Post Office. He consulted his general practitioner, anti-tetanus serum was given without an adequate test dose, and nine days later he developed encephalitis and was left with physical and mental disabilities. He

* (1909) 2 KB 820; 78 LJ (KB) 958.
† (1951) 1 All ER 574; 2 KB 343 CA.
‡ (1952) 2 All ER 125; 2 QB 852 CA.
§ (1950) WN 553; 94 SJ 758 HL.
¶ (1954) 2 All ER 131. 2 QB 66 CA.
‖ (1957) 2 All ER 118. 1 WLR 582.

sued the Post Office and the general practitioner. The Court of Appeal upheld the trial court in exonerating the GP on the grounds that his failure to administer an adequate test dose was irrelevant to the development of encephalitis. The Post Office were found liable, it being forseeable that having cut his leg the plaintiff would attend his doctor and receive anti-tetanic serum which directly caused the disabilities*.

The standard of care enforced by the Courts is exemplified in Wells *v* Surrey AHA†, in which case the Judge took the view that it was not enough that a patient was asked four or five times whether she would wish to be sterilised when it was decided to proceed to caesarian section, and that her husband was summoned from his work to discuss the matter with her. The doctor was negligent in failing to advise that the sterilisation could, if so desired, be done at a later date, and that if the patient had not previously considered it, it might be better not to make an immediate decision.

Finally, in a judgment which will undoubtedly save many women from unnecessary caesarian section, the House of Lords decided in the case of Whitehouse *v* Jordan and Another‡, that a senior registrar was not negligent in his conduct of a trial of forceps prior to proceeding to caesarian section. The baby was born with brain damage which the plaintiff sought to relate to the registrar having pulled too hard and for too long.

Diagnosis

Failure to make an accurate diagnosis is not in itself evidence of negligence, and in order to make the doctor liable the plaintiff must prove that the faulty diagnosis was the result of failure to exercise reasonable skill and care. In the case of Stevens *v* Bermondsey and Southwark Group HMC§, the plaintiff sustained injury as a result of being thrown from his bicycle due to the negligence of a local authority's road sweeper. Following medical advice as to the extent of his injuries, the plaintiff settled his claim against the local authority for £125, £50 of which was in respect of pain and suffering. Subse-

* Robinson *v* Post Office (1974). 1 WLR 1176.

† Wells *v* Surrey AHA. *The Times*, 29 July 1978.

‡ Whitehouse *v* Jordan (1980). 1 All ER 650. *The Times*, 18 December 1980. *Lancet*, 17 January 1981, 167.

§ (1963) *The Times*, 16 May.

quently, it was revealed that the plaintiff's condition was more serious than had first been believed and he claimed damages for negligence against the defendant hospital. In disallowing that part of the plaintiff's claim for damages which related to lost compensation which might otherwise have been obtained from the local authority, the Judge said that a doctor's duty was limited to the sphere of medicine and had nothing to do with the sphere of legal liability unless he examined with an eye to liability. Unless there were special circumstances, he was not required to contemplate or foresee any question connected with a third party's liability to his patient. This is not the place to go further into this point, but it may be that any similar case coming before the Courts will be viewed in the light of Hedley Byrne *v* Heller* which could lead to a different decision.

Failure to take steps to diagnose a fracture is perhaps the most common of all allegations of medical negligence, and undoubtedly the bone most commonly involved is the scaphoid. A casualty officer saw a patient complaining of pain over the dorsum of the right hand following a fall, and finding no evidence of bone injury, diagnosed a sprain, applied strapping and advised the patient to return in two days. When seen again the patient stated that there was some improvement, was given a crepe bandage and told to return if progress was not satisfactory. He continued to work but returned to the hospital about five weeks later as the hand and wrist were painful. A fracture of the scaphoid was then suspected and confirmed by X-ray. A claim was duly lodged alleging negligence, and in particular stating that an X-ray shoud have been taken when the patient first attended. The opinion of an orthopaedic surgeon was to the effect that the delay in immobilising the fracture had not led to any permanent ill effect, but that the rate of union was somewhat slower than it might have been had the injury been diagnosed earlier and the wrist immediately immobilised. In such circumstances a settlement was negotiated.

Perhaps the classic case of missed fractures is that of Wood *v* Thurston†, where a casualty officer, receiving no report of an accident and faced with a patient who had perhaps a dulled reaction to pain due to drink, failed to carry out an adequate examination and overlooked eighteen fractured ribs. Misled by the lack of

* (1963) 3 WLR 101; (1963) 2 All ER 575; (1964) AC 465.

† (1951) *The Times*, 25 May.

history and absence of complaint, the doctor did not use a stethoscope and was duly held to have been negligent.

While it is seldom possible to avoid liability when a fracture has been missed, circumstances occasionally make such a case defensible. A provisionally registered house surgeon standing in on casualty duty was called to see a patient who had injured his hip in a road accident. He examined the hip and an X-ray was taken though no bone injury was observed. Later the films were examined by a consultant radiologist who reported a mass with a calcified periphery at the upper end of the shaft of the femur, and a portion of bone detached from some part of the neck. No complete fracture of the neck was seen. The patient was instructed to return home and to rest for a few days. Eighteen days later he was again examined; it was found that he was unable to walk on his right leg and there was some wasting of the muscles. A further X-ray was then taken which disclosed an impacted fracture of the neck of the right femur with rotation of the distal portion. An operation for insertion of a Smith-Petersen pin followed, and after convalescence the patient was back at work within four months. A year after the operation the pin was removed, and eight months later X-ray showed aseptic necrosis of the head of the femur which led to an osteotomy being performed with a very good result.

Three years after the accident negligence was alleged against the house surgeon and liability was denied, it being contended that it could not be negligent for a house surgeon to fail to diagnose that which a consultant was subsequently unable to discern. In the event, a very small amount was paid by the hospital in settlement, as there was some question regarding the adequacy of the films and the allegation of negligence against the house surgeon was not pursued.

Whether negligence has occurred or not depends upon the degree of skill and care brought to bear. In the case of Newton *v* Newton's Model Laundry*, a doctor had failed to diagnose fractures of the nose, wrist and patella. In respect of the two former fractures his failure was not considered to amount to negligence, but he was adjudged negligent in respect of his failure to diagnose the fractured patella.

In the realm of diagnosis the casualty officer and, even more, the provisionally registered house surgeon or house physician standing in on casualty duty, is particularly at risk without at times having easy access to more experienced opinion. One casualty officer found

* (1959) CLY 2256; *The Times*, 3 November.

himself faced with a baby aged thirteen months, with a note from a general practitioner requesting X-ray films of the chest because of a history that the child was suspected of having inhaled a crumb. There was no respiratory distress but a film was taken and the casualty officer noting nothing abnormal wrote to the practitioner and referred the patient back to him. The baby's cough became worse during the evening and the next morning the consultant radiologist viewed the film. He immediately diagnosed a collapse of part of one lung and prompt attempts were made to contact the general practitioner and have the baby admitted to hospital. At the same time as these events were taking place, however, the baby had a paroxysm of coughing and died. Autopsy revealed that death was due to respiratory obstruction caused by an orange pip lodged at the carina. A claim for damages followed and it was felt that the appearances of the film were such that they should at least have led the casualty officer to seek more experienced opinion, and a settlement was therefore negotiated.

A provisionally registered house physician on casualty duty was called to see a man of late middle age brought in by ambulance, the patient stating that he had collapsed. The doctor found that only two hours earlier the patient had been in the casualty department when the casualty officer had examined and discharged him, finding nothing abnormal. There was also a history that this patient had, about a month previously, twice in the same day presented himself at the casualty department the worse for drink, and been taken away by the police. A rapid examination was carried out, a slight bruise of the right side of the scalp noted, the patient was detained in the department for an hour and then sent home by ambulance. The ambulance men returned to say that they had had difficulty in getting the patient into his home and that his speech had not been normal. The doctor took no action on this information and a short while later a general practitioner telephoned to ask about the patient's condition saying that his wife had made an enquiry. The house physician assured the practitioner that he had found nothing abnormal. About five hours after the patient had been sent home he was brought back to the hospital, deeply unconscious, by a doctor working for a deputising organisation, with a provisional diagnosis of pontine haemorrhage. The patient's condition deteriorated and he died some seven hours later not having regained consciousness. Post mortem examination showed an extra-dural haemorrhage, and in due course negligence was alleged against both the casualty officer and the house physician.

On consideration of the case it was felt that it might well have been reasonable for the casualty officer to discharge the patient in the first place, but the fact that he was brought back by ambulance with a vague history of collapse and had a bruise of the scalp should have led the house physician either to detain the patient, X-ray the skull, or seek the advice of some senior person. Further, the failure to initiate action on receipt of the ambulance men's report and again following the enquiry from the GP was felt to make a denial of liability untenable. In all probability it was too late to take remedial action when the patient was finally brought back to the hospital and failure to consider the possibility of extra-dural haemorrhage at that time was therefore irrelevant. A Court hearing, however, could only have damaged the house physician's reputation, and a settlement had to be negotiated.

Treatment

Treatment, of course, offers even greater scope than diagnosis for negligent acts and omissions, and the following small selection of cases will speak eloquently enough.

Penicillin

A casualty officer passing through his department was asked by the sister to look at a patient who had a laceration of his left forearm sutured in the hospital a month or so before. The patient had returned with signs of infection, and remarking that he would probably need penicillin the doctor passed on his way to attend to an accident case. Having dealt with this matter he returned to see the patient and found the sister had already given penicillin, although it was discovered that the patient's card was clearly marked 'sensitive to penicillin'. Sensitivity reactions, not of great severity, ensued but when allegations of negligence were made they were clearly incontrovertible and a settlement was negotiated, responsibility being accepted equally between the protection society on behalf of the doctor and the hospital on behalf of the sister.

There is little doubt that, in the absence of exceptional circumstances it would be adjudged negligent not to ask about sensitivity before prescribing penicillin. The case of Chin Keow *v* Government of Malaysia* was one in which a doctor injected procaine penicillin

* Chin Keow *v* Government of Malaysia (1967). 1 WER 813.

and the patient died within the hour. The patient's card carried the warning 'Allergic to penicillin' and the Privy Council advised that the doctor had been negligent in failing to make due enquiry.

Blood

Blood is, without question, a hazardous form of therapy in its own right, but only too often human failing increases the hazards. Causes of error abound. One hospital instituted what was doubtless thought to be a foolproof system at the time of its inception and involved no fewer than four people carrying out the necessary checks to ensure that the right blood got into the right patient. In the light of what happened subsequently, it can only be assumed that all four took the view that three checks were quite sufficient.

Doctors will doubtless never name their daughters 'Melina', but this name has been used, and house surgeons should not, on being told by nurse that a certain bottle of blood is for Melina, assume without checking that it is intended for a person bleeding per rectum who happened, on the occasion in question, to be lying in the bed next to Melina.

A middle-aged female was admitted to hospital for treatment of an oesophageal stricture caused by her having accidentally swallowed caustic soda eighteen months previously. It was intended to resect the affected portion of oesophagus and replace it with a colon graft. The patient's blood was grouped and a blood group determination form sent to the ward. Reports from the laboratory were stuck on a card from below upwards, each report overlapping the previous one, so that the patient's name appeared on the top of the card but would be obscured when one turned back recent reports to look at earlier ones. The insertion of reports was normally the duty of a registered nurse, but it appeared in this case that it must have been undertaken by some unqualified person. All went well at operation until the chest was opened when the carotid pulse became impalpable and three pints of blood were ordered. When the particulars on the bottles had been checked against the blood group determination form in the patient's case sheet, the blood was administered. Later in the operation the patient's condition worsened, and a further three pints were given after a similar check. By the end of the operation the patient's condition was fair and she recovered consciousness before her return to the ward. In view of the possibility of oozing from cut surfaces, a seventh pint was commenced and two hours after the operation more was ordered. On this occasion the patient's name was taken not from the blood group determination form but from the front of the patient's notes, though the blood group itself and the reference number were taken from the form. It was then discovered that the name did not tally with the blood group and reference number, and enquiries were made. It was found that there were two patients of the same surname, but different first names, in the ward under the house surgeon who had been responsible for ordering the blood on the first occasion. These two patients had been admitted and their blood grouped at about the same time, and it was found that the determination forms had been transposed. The house surgeon immediately informed the surgeon concerned, a replacement transfusion of some six pints was carried out, but after an initial improvement the patient's condition deteriorated and she died some nine hours after the end of the operation. When the inevitable claim followed it was thought that the prime responsibility rested on the hospital authorities in respect of the nurse who placed the incorrect blood group determination form in the patient's folder. At the same time it had to be admitted that the house surgeon, in ordering the blood, had a duty to check the patient's name and number on the form with those on the card upon which the forms were stuck, or on the front of the patient's notes. The very fact that he had admitted two patients with the same surname to the same ward should, it was felt, have made him particularly careful in this respect. The hospital authority put forward the view that, as they issued a pamphlet which laid it down that it was the duty of resident medical officers to see that full clinical notes were recorded and all special reports attached thereto, the responsibility was entirely that of the house surgeon. This view was not acceptable to the protection society and eventually a settlement was reached to which the society contributed one third.

A further hazard put in the way of unsuspecting residents concerned a radiologist who, being particularly interested in one facet of his specialty, labelled certain patients' notes Group A and Group B, which classification was duly stamped on the front of the patients' records. It was, of course, not long before someone assumed that this meant precisely what most members of the profession would take it to mean.

Invasive techniques

Minor surgical procedures are not always as free from risk as the uninitiated might imagine, as a house physician found when instructed to aspirate the air from the pleural cavity of a girl aged eleven with a spontaneous pneumothorax. The only instruction given by the consultant was that the needle should be inserted into the broadest part of the chest and although the house physician said that while she had performed ordinary chest aspirations, she had not previously dealt with a pneumothorax, the consultant did not consider personal supervision to be necessary. The house physician consulted a recent textbook, selected a wide-bore needle and proposed to insert this in the mid axillary line just below the seventh rib, as advised in the textbook. The needle was fixed in position with the point just within the chest wall by a collodion gauze pad and adhesive strapping around the needle, anchoring it to the skin. Satisfactory under-water drainage was established and the child was visited several times by the house physician throughout the afternoon and evening. The following morning the patient suddenly collapsed, and X-ray examination confirmed that there was fluid in the chest which the consultant thought was probably blood. The child was placed in an oxygen tent, a thoracic surgeon expressed the view that there was a haemothorax but no haemopericardium, and after improvement for a day or two the patient had a sudden convulsion and died. At the subsequent inquest evidence was given by a pathologist that the cause of death was 'puncture of pericardium and heart . . .'. He indicated the position of the puncture wound as being about half an inch in front of the anterior axillary line. It was evident that several factors had contributed to the fatality, namely the insertion of the needle in front of the mid-axillary line, the length of the needle (9 cm), its long bevel, and the method of anchorage which permitted it to penetrate further into the chest cavity than was intended. It was not surprising, therefore, that a Writ was issued claiming damages for this most unhappy accident. In due course a settlement had to be negotiated to which the protection organisations representing the consultant and the house physician contributed in equal proportions.

Tetanus

Tetanus prophylaxis is a matter on which a clearly understood policy is essential if tragedies are to be avoided. A boy was brought to a hospital department having suffered a wound of the face. The casualty officer who saw him ordered a nurse to suture the wound and give tetanus toxoid. Infection supervened, and five days later the casualty officer saw the patient again when he ordered the stitches to be removed and penicillin to be prescribed. The following day another casualty officer explored the wound and removed from it two pieces of wood which he handed to the boy's mother. Two days later the boy was admitted to hospital, the next morning tetanus was diagnosed and, despite transfer to a special unit, the patient died six weeks after the original injury. Following an inquest, a claim was lodged alleging negligence and it was apparent that the actions of the casualty officer who originally saw the patient could not be defended. This conclusion was reached because, whatever the merits of tetanus toxoid, basic surgical principles as well as those of tetanus prophylaxis require that wounds receive adequate toilet and debridement. Further investigation, moreover, showed that neither of the casualty officers had a clear understanding of departmental policy in respect of tetanus prophylaxis, ignorance partly due to inadequate instruction. A settlement was therefore negotiated in which the protection organisation to which the consultant in charge of the casualty department belonged contributed. Had adequate surgical care been combined with toxoid and adequate antibiotic cover, or alternatively, had antitetanic serum—the boy was unprotected against tetanus—been given, this case would probably have been defensible, for doctors are not obliged to follow any particular course of therapy and are fully entitled to follow any course which has the support of a responsible section of the profession.

Plaster of Paris

If would-be orthopaedic house surgeons wish to spare themselves unnecessary worry, they might consider rejecting jobs where they find that the Chief operates on Fridays. As the best manure is the farmer's boot, so the best protection against the ills which flow from overtight plasters is the Chief's round, and a remarkably high proportion of such cases occur when the Chief is away for the weekend, having operated on a Friday.

An eleven-year-old boy fractured the lower end of his left radius and ulna and, following reduction under general anaesthetic, a plaster slab was applied and the child's mother was asked to bring him back the following day. When he attended he was seen by a recently qualified house surgeon who considered the splint to be loose and, therefore, asked the sister to apply a crepe bandage. The house surgeon did not actually watch the bandaging but was satisfied with the result before sending the boy home with specific directions to keep the fingers moving. No adult accompanied the boy on this occasion, though on the previous day his mother had been told that he should attend on the following day and again a week later. Three days later, the boy was brought back to the department by his sister, his hand blue and swollen, and he was complaining of pain at the elbow and wrist. The house surgeon saw him, removed the plaster slab, and ordered its replacement by a full padded plaster to include the elbow joint. The plaster was split, and his sister was told that the boy must attend again the following day.

When he failed to arrive, the house surgeon told the casualty officer about her anxiety, but did nothing further. The next day, i.e. two days after the last attendance, the child came back to hospital very ill, in great pain, his hand black, with the skin blistered. An above-elbow amputation was found to be necessary. Within a few weeks a claim was lodged seeking damages against the hospital authority. On the doctor's behalf it was stressed that the hospital administration appeared to be at fault in permitting such an inexperienced doctor to assume responsibilities for which she was quite untrained. For the hospital it was stated that the doctor's failure to make sure that the crepe bandage was not applied too tightly, and her failure to consult a senior colleague before ordering the replacement of the plaster slab with a full plaster could not be ignored. Shortly before the matter was due to go to trial the patient's solicitors intimated that a settlement might be reached for a sum very much less than that claimed and this was duly concluded, it being agreed that the hospital should contribute eighty per cent and the doctor's protection society twenty per cent.

In a teaching hospital, the following unusual accident concerned with plaster of Paris occurred. A provisionally registered house surgeon was intending to change a full plaster which had been applied in the treatment of a Colles fracture. The patient made no comment while the plaster was being removed, but it was then found that a wound five inches long had been caused by the plaster shears on the volar aspect of the forearm, penetrating down to the deep fascia. This was sutured under local anaesthesia and another plaster applied. When the patient was seen the next day by the orthopaedic consultant the arm was found to be satisfactory, but a spontaneous rupture of the tendon of the extensor pollicis longus had occurred. This was duly operated upon and at operation it was found that the proximal part of the wound caused by the plaster shears had failed to heal, and this was re-sutured. Some six months later the patient developed in the same wrist a carpal tunnel syndrome which necessitated further operation. Although it was obvious that the wound in the forearm was caused by the plaster shears, it was quite fortuitous that the patient had the misfortune to suffer two of the complications which sometimes follow a Colles fracture. The spontaneous rupture of the extensor pollicis longus is thought generally to be due to an interference with the blood supply of the tendon at the site of the fracture, and the carpal tunnel syndrome to result from fibrosis of the anterior annular ligament. Not unexpectedly, the patient attributed these complications to the laceration of the forearm, and proceedings were instituted against the hospital authority and the house surgeon. While it was felt that the greater liability here lay upon the house surgeon, it was agreed that the hospital authority should contribute, inasmuch as the plaster shears then in use were of a defective design and had been changed immediately following the mishap. Liability for the complications of the fracture was denied, and in due course a reasonable settlement was achieved in respect of the laceration alone.

Drug Identification

However capable the nursing staff may be, a doctor is responsible for taking all reasonable steps to assure himself in respect of any medicament he may use. The simplest, quickest, and most essential step is to read the label.

A patient was admitted to hospital with severe anal pain for which no cause was apparent. A house surgeon, on the instructions of a registrar, injected proctocaine into the anal sphincter and, as there was marked tenderness, proposed to insert Xylocaine jelly into the anal canal. A tube of the jelly was requested and brought from the theatre. The house surgeon read the name Lignocaine on the label but it was found that the jelly could not be expelled from the tube. At this moment visiting commenced in the ward and the houseman decided to have the patient taken to the theatre where he used a tube of jelly handed to him by an experienced sister, though subsequently he had no certain recollection of asking again for Xylocaine nor of examining the label on the tube. A few hours later a house physician was called to see the patient who had developed convulsions. No firm diagnosis was made, but paraldehyde was given with good effect and, when further muscle twitchings occurred about two hours later, a second dose was administered. Later that evening the house surgeon was called to see the patient and found her dead.

Following an autopsy, analysis showed that the body contained a very large quantity of Nupercaine which was considered to be the cause of death. Investigation showed that the tube used by the house surgeon in the theatre had contained four per cent Nupercaine jelly, which was made up in the hospital pharmacy and packed in tubes identical with those used for Lignocaine. It appeared that the house surgeon had placed the nozzle of the tube in the anal canal and expelled an indefinite quantity of the jelly. When a claim was duly lodged a settlement had to be explored, and having regard to the action of the hospital authority which permitted tubes of Lignocaine and Nupercaine, identical in appearance, to be kept together in the theatre, this was contributed in equal proportions by the hospital authority and the house surgeon's protection society.

Foreign Bodies

A young man riding his motorcycle on a speedway track had the misfortune to have the driving chain snap and strike the back of his left thigh. A deep laceration was inflicted which was in due course cleaned and sutured by a casualty officer. Antitetanic serum and penicillin were administered and the patient given a letter to take to a hospital near his home. Some six months later it was heard that the patient had been referred to another hospital on account of a persistent sinus at the site of the injury, and exploration of the wound had revealed three links of motorcycle chain embedded in the muscle. Once again a settlement had to be negotiated.

Diathermy Burns

Burns can result from many causes when diathermy is being used; pads drying out, short circuits, worn flex, flex damaged by towel clips, are all possible causes and are matters over which the doctor has perhaps little control. The same, however, could not be said of the case where a woman, prior to cauterisation of the cervix, was placed in the lithotomy position and the vagina swabbed out with Cetavlon followed by spirit. A speculum was placed in position, the cervix seized with volsellum forceps and the diathermy electrode approximated to the vulva. A spark and flash of flame followed, the excess spirit having soaked into the towels beneath the patient's buttocks which were extensively burned, and two skin grafting operations were required. A claim followed and was, of course, no more defensible than the case of the surgeon who inadvertently used spirit prior to cauterising anal warts.

Instrument Burns

Heat sterilisation carries an inherent risk because substantial metal objects store heat. It is by no means uncommon for an instrument after sterilisation to be dipped in a cold solution and passed then to the operator who places it in position, later finding that it has caused a burn. In one such case a registrar performing a minor gynaecological operation was handed a speculum which he used, and knew of no mishap until subsequently it was discovered that the patient had sustained a burn of the buttock measuring 3 in × 2 in from contact with the weighted end. Skin grafting and a six week stay in hospital proved necessary. This type of burn is also not infrequently caused by the hot handle of dental forceps pressing against the lip. The scar, passing as it does across the muco-cutaneous junction, may cause severe disfigurement for which heavy damages can be claimed.

Retained Swabs

These are perhaps the classic cases of negligence, and while in the vast majority of cases no defence is possible, circumstances can arise in which such a mishap is not indicative of negligence.

A woman involved in a motor accident fractured eight ribs and, when taken to hospital, the surgeon realised that this was just the type of case in which a delayed rupture of the spleen might occur. The patient was, on this account, supervised with the greatest care over the next few days and during the afternoon of the third day after the accident she suddenly collapsed with severe internal haemorrhage. Following resuscitation an emergency operation was performed when the diagnosis of ruptured spleen was confirmed. The abdominal cavity contained a vast quantity of blood which was mopped and sucked out as well as possible in the circumstances to permit the splenic pedicle to be visualised. The operation was made more difficult by the patient's obesity and the need for speed, and the point was reached when the pulse and blood pressure became unrecordable. As soon as the spleen had been removed the other abdominal organs were rapidly examined and the site searched for swabs both visually and manually. At this point it was not certain whether the patient was dead or alive, and the theatre sister reporting the swab count as correct, the incision was closed as speedily as possible and the patient returned to the ward. She recovered very satisfactorily and was discharged from hospital sixteen days after the operation. Unfortunately, during the following month a swab was removed from the abdomen at another hospital, and this was quickly followed by a Writ alleging negligence against the hospital authority. The view taken by the Medical Protection Society was that this was a case which must be defended at all costs. The surgeon had exercised great care and displayed outstanding skill and there could be no question but that in the hands of a less able man the patient must inevitably have died. At the crucial moment the surgeon made the right decision and sewed up, and were a Court to consider such action negligent they would inevitably thereby place the lives of any persons who might subsequently be in a similar position in jeopardy. It was, however, the view of the hospital authority that the patient would succeed against them and they therefore insisted on reaching a settlement to which the protection society refused to make any contribution.

Assistance from Nurses

Welcome as is the assistance a nurse can often give in a matter not entirely within her sphere, and understandable as is her desire to give such assistance, the possible added dangers to the patient must be recognised and guarded against.

A patient was being operated on for varicose veins by a surgical registrar assisted by a house surgeon who was unfortunately called away to attend an emergency, his place being taken by a nurse. Impressed by the efficiency of his helper and the competent way in which she secured bleeding points with artery forceps when the skin incision was made, the registrar told her to continue to apply forceps to any bleeding point which presented. The dissection of the veins did not prove easy and in the popliteal fossa, where there was much scar tissue, difficulty arose in separating two large varices from the lateral popliteal nerve to which they were closely adherent. During the course of the dissection one of the varices was ruptured and as the surgeon turned to get a swab from the trolley he asked the nurse to control the bleeding. Instead of applying a swab as he had intended the nurse applied a pair of Spencer Wells, and unfortunately included the popliteal nerve. The error was recognised immediately and the forceps removed, but the resulting footdrop was still marked more than a year after the operation. The Writ which was issued led to a settlement being arrived at, both the hospital authority and the Medical Protection Society contributing.

Delegation of Responsibility

The natural wish of a doctor to accept ever increasing responsibility should be tempered by prudence and a realisation of his limitations. An emergency operation is seldom an appropriate occasion on which to leave a junior to undertake a procedure with which he is not entirely familiar.

A patient in a hospital for treatment of his peptic ulcer suffered severe haemorrhage and the consultant surgeon was called in. Operation was decided upon, and this was commenced in the early hours of the morning. Having mobilised the stomach and closed the duodenal stump, the surgeon left his registrar to complete the anastomosis of the stomach remnant to the small intestine. The patient made normal progress and, when seen in out-patients five weeks after the operation, seemed well apart from occasional attacks of diarrhoea. A few months later, however, the patient, who had returned to Ireland, was investigated for loss of weight. A barium meal demonstrated that the small bowel appeared to be only a foot long. It was thought that the bowel must have been removed at operation and contact was made with the consultant who had operated in the first place. The latter stated that no bowel had been removed and advised an urgent laparotomy which, in the event, showed that the stomach remnant had been anastomosed to the lower end of the ileum. The claim which was duly lodged was settled in equal proportions by the protection organisations of which the consultant and registrar were members.

Communications

The palest ink is said to be better than the most acute memory, but this is true only if one takes the trouble to read it. 'Hello Michael,' said the anaesthetist in his most reassuring tone but, because his premedicated seven-year-old patient did not insist that his name was Timothy, and the anaesthetist thinking that he knew the child by sight did not take the precaution of checking the notes, the operation intended for Michael was performed, greatly to the displeasure of the parents of Timothy.

A consultant surgeon saw, in his private consulting rooms, a child with a recurrent umbilical hernia. He advised further surgery and as soon as the parents had departed, telephoned his secretary at the hospital requesting that the child be put on the waiting list. The secretary duly completed the admission form on which she entered the condition requiring treatment as 'bilateral inguinal herniae'. At no time did the surgeon send any written confirmation to the hospital.

Some three months later the child was admitted and examined by the house surgeon whose notes referred to bilateral inguinal herniae and included no reference to an umbilical hernia. The surgeon saw the patient in the anaesthetic room, checked the notes with the identity tag and proceeded to operate, finding bilateral inguinal sacs. The following day a haemorrhage on the left side necessitated exploration of the wound by a resident surgical officer who ligated a small artery. Four days after the operation the child's mother noticed that the umbilicus had not been touched and the error then came to light.

The surgeon saw the parents, expressed his regret for the mistake, but pointed out that the presence of the inguinal sacs meant that herniae might have developed and required operation at a later date. The child was subsequently discharged with an appointment to attend out-patients in four weeks. Three weeks later, however, the child's general practitioner contacted the surgeon to say that the patient was limping and that he had found weakness of the quadriceps and an area of impaired sensation over the anterior aspect of the thigh. The surgeon concluded that the femoral nerve must have been damaged by himself and not by the resident surgical officer, for he recollected that there had been some troublesome bleeding near the internal abdominal vein which he had controlled by under-running the vessel and he considered that he must, at that time, have included the femoral nerve in the ligature. Subsequently, the child underwent a further operation by another surgeon when the femoral nerve was found to end in a neuroma just above the inguinal ligament, rendering its repair impossible.

When a claim was lodged it had to be agreed that such a sequence of events was indefensible. Apart from the unfortunate accident with the femoral nerve, the method of communication between surgeon and hospital must inevitably, it was felt, be regarded by a Court as negligent. Having regard to the gross wasting of the quadriceps, some wasting of the calf muscles, the asymmetry of the legs and the effects that this would presumably cause in later life, a settlement was only effected by payment of a very substantial sum.

8 Courts and Legal Procedure

There are perhaps but two beliefs concerning the law common to most doctors. Knowledge of its asinine quality is universal, and it is generally appreciated that there is a clear distinction in tempo between a surgeon faced with an acute abdomen and a solicitor served with a Writ in the Chancery Division of the High Court. Doctors involved in legal proceedings frequently feel it necessary to enquire as to what, if anything, is happening, and this chapter aims at explaining something of what is occupying the solicitor while the law moves in its mysterious way.

Civil Procedure

The only civil courts with which a doctor is likely to be involved are the County Court and the Queen's Bench Division of the High Court. In claims based in tort and contract the County Court is limited to trying actions where the claim does not exceed £5000. The County Court procedure is similar to but not identical with that of the Queen's Bench Division which is discussed in this chapter.

The County Courts are presided over by the County Court Judges, addressed as 'Your Honour', who are barristers of not less than ten years' standing. They are assisted by Registrars who act as Chief Clerk to the Court, with authority to try minor cases which may subsequently be appealed to the Judge. The name 'County Court' is a misnomer, for there are many County Courts in each county.

The County Court also deals with small claims and a reference is commonly made to the Small Claims Court. This is misleading as the small claims are made in the County Court normally without the assistance of legal advice and representation, as it is only in rare cases that legal costs can be recovered. These cases are usually heard by the Registrar and claims can be made for sums up to £500.

Turning to the High Court, there are three Divisions, Queen's Bench, Chancery and Family.

The Queen's Bench Division deals with actions in contract and tort. It is comprised of the Lord Chief Justice and a number of Judges, who must, prior to appointment, be barristers of at least ten years' standing and are addressed as 'My Lord'. The jurisdiction of the Court is unlimited in amount.

The Queen's Bench Masters, who are appointed by the Lord Chancellor from practising barristers or solicitors of not less than ten years' standing, deal with the preparatory work necessary for a case before it comes on for trial. An appeal can be made from the decision of the Master to a Judge in Chambers.

There are ten steps in a civil action:

1 Writ
2 Acknowledgment of Service
3 Pleadings
4 Discovery
5 Summons for Directions
6 Setting down for trial
7 Trial
8 Judgment
9 Execution
10 Taxation of costs

A plaintiff wishing to bring an action should issue and serve proceedings within the period prescribed by the Limitation Acts. In the case of personal injury actions the Writ should be issued within three years from the date of the cause of action, or if later, three years from the date the plaintiff became aware he had a cause for action.

Where the plaintiff is under a disability because he is an infant or a mental patient, the period does not start to run until the end of the disability, that is in the case of infants from their eighteenth birthday.

However, the Limitation Act 1980 gives the Court the power to extend the prescribed periods in certain circumstances, so preventing a claim from being statute barred.

Writ

The Writ is served on the defendant requiring him to enter an Acknowledgment of Service, stating also that should he fail to do so judgment may be entered against him. The Writ will either be endorsed with an indication of the nature of the plaintiff's claim against the defendant, or be a specially endorsed Writ, which means that the Statement of Claim is included on the Writ, giving short details of the plaintiff's claim.

The Writ must be served within twelve months of the date of its being issued by the Royal Courts of Justice in the Strand, or a District Registry, that is, a branch of the High Court. The Court can grant leave for renewal of the Writ, so providing a further twelve months for service. Nowadays Writs are generally served by post, but in view of postal difficulties the Court will set aside a judgment entered in default of an Acknowledgment of Service if satisfied that the Writ did not come to the notice of the defendant. The Court will permit service out of the jurisdiction in appropriate cases.

Acknowledgment of Service

A defendant upon being served with a Writ has fourteen days within which to file an Acknowledgment of Service. A form of Acknowledgment of Service must accompany the Writ that is served upon the defendant, and explains how and to which Court the defendant may file the Acknowledgment. A copy duly stamped by the Court is returned to the defendant or his solicitor and the Court forwards another copy to the plaintiff or his solicitor. The defendant must state on the Acknowledgment of Service whether he intends to contest the proceedings. If the defendant fails to file an Acknowledgment of Service, or omits to state his intention to contest the proceedings, he will be taken as having expressed the desire not to defend and the plaintiff may then enter judgment.

Pleadings

The purpose of pleadings is to define the essential points at issue between the parties.

Statement of Claim

The Statement of Claim if not endorsed on the Writ should normally be served within fourteen days of filing the Acknowledgment of Service. It consists of a summary of facts and contentions upon which the plaintiff proposes to rely, and in addition it details the relief and/or remedy sought against the defendant. It is customary for the Statement of Claim to commence by setting out in chronological sequence the occurrences which gave rise to the action, then particularise the manner in which the defendant's acts or omissions are alleged to have made him liable to the plaintiff and to conclude by claiming damages which may be general and/or special. General damages are claimed to cover intangible loss such as pain, suffering, loss of amenities, shock, loss of expectation of life, inconvenience, and stress such as the prospect of undergoing a further operation. Special damages are those that can be particularised, and substantiated by documentary or oral evidence, such as loss of earnings, replacement of property, and medical expenses. A plaintiff can claim for private medical treatment, but the Pearson Report, that is the report of the Royal Commission on Civil Liability and Compensation for Personal Injury, recommended that the cost of private treatment should be allowed only when justified as being 'reasonable on medical grounds', and legislation to this end is envisaged.

The Defence

Following service of the Statement of Claim, the defendant, if he proposes to defend the action, serves his Defence within 14 days, unless the Statement of Claim accompanied the Writ, in which case the period is 28 days. Should he fail to do so the plaintiff may apply to enter judgment. The Defence is a document in which the defendant states the facts on which he proposes to rely with a view to resisting the plaintiff's claim. Each alleged fact in the Statement of Claim is dealt with in order and the defendant must deal with every material fact alleged. The Defence may traverse, confess and avoid, or object on point of law. A traverse may deny or give a statement of non-admission. In the event that the Defence does not include a denial or statement of non-admission, the defendant is taken to accept and admit a fact. To confess and avoid is to admit the facts alleged, but at the same time to assert that additional facts have the effect of nullifying or altering the implications which the plaintiff seeks to assert. In a case where a doctor was sued for assault it was alleged in the Statement of Claim that he had seized the plaintiff and forcibly propelled him through the surgery door. The Defence admitted that this had occurred but added that the doctor only took this action after the plaintiff had refused to vacate the premises when asked to do so, and furthermore that no excess force had been used.

An objection on point of law in the Defence is an assertion that the facts alleged by the plaintiff in the Statement of Claim do not give him any right of action or in any way render the defendant liable to him. In such case the defendant may apply to have the case struck out as showing no reasonable cause of action.

The Defence may be accompanied by a Counterclaim by the defendant against the plaintiff, and/or a Set Off by which the defendant admits part or all of the plaintiff's claim and states his willingness to set off a certain sum which he alleges is owed to him by the plaintiff.

Reply to Defence and Defence to Counterclaim

The Reply deals with the facts contained in the Defence. The defendant can proceed to judgment on the Counterclaim in the event that no Defence is served to it.

Payment into Court

In many cases the defendant may accept that he is, to some extent, indebted to the plaintiff, yet feel that the claim made is excessive. In such circumstances a payment into Court will be considered, and any sum paid into Court must include interest calculated up until the date of payment in. Such a payment is not mentioned in any documents put before the Judge, so that if the case is pursued to trial the Judge will have no knowledge of it. The plaintiff on being served with Notice of Payment can accept the sum at any time up to the date of the trial, but after the expiry of 21 days from the service of the Notice of Payment this can only be done with the leave of the Court, which can in these circumstances order the plaintiff to pay the defendant's costs from the date of payment in. If he accepts it in full settlement of his claim, the action is then brought to a conclusion with the agreement or the taxation of the plaintiff's costs. If it is not accepted the case comes to trial, and a successful plaintiff may be awarded an amount greater than, equal to, or less than the sum previously paid into Court. While the question of the award of costs—a far from insignificant item in most actions—is at the entire discretion of the Judge trying the action, it is usual for costs to be awarded so that the defendant is ordered to pay the plaintiff's costs where the sum awarded exceeds the payment into Court. Where, on the other hand, the sum awarded to the plaintiff is equal to or less than the amount paid into Court by the defendant, then it is customary for the Judge to award costs incurred subsequent to the payment into Court to the defendant, i.e. the plaintiff is compelled to pay not only his own but also the defendant's costs as from the date of the payment into Court.

The plaintiff may at any time after the Writ has been served on the defendant and the time limited for him to acknowledge service has expired, apply to the Court for an interim payment. An order will be made if the Court is satisfied that liability is not in dispute or that if the action proceeded to trial the plaintiff would obtain judgment for substantial damages. The Court will order the defendant to make a payment of such an amount as it thinks just, not exceeding a reasonable proportion of the damages which are likely to be recovered after taking into account any relevant contributory negligence.

Discovery

To assist in confining the issue between the parties and to help to minimise costs, it is obviously helpful if each party is able to view all relevant documents. In general, each party to an action is required to supply the other party or parties with a list of the documents in his possession and to allow these to be viewed and copied. Certain documents a party is not obliged to disclose, and in this case the reason for non-disclosure must be stated. It is then open to the other party or parties to make application to the Master for an Order of Discovery in respect of the documents undisclosed, and the Master will rule as to whether the applicant is so entitled. The effect of non-disclosure of documents may be that the action is dismissed, or that the Defence is struck out and judgment entered for the plaintiff.

Apart from the value in saving time and costs in the actual discovery of documents, the fact that such documents will have to be disclosed should litigation ensue will often influence the conduct of the parties prior to action. Solicitors representing a patient aggrieved regarding her treatment in hospital may ask for a copy of the hospital notes. If there exist obvious grounds for action, such as an operation on the wrong side, then there is nothing to be gained in refusing to disclose, for the patient's claim is indefensible and will certainly be pursued. Where, however, the patient's allegations are thought to be without substance then the request will probably be refused in the hope, slight perhaps, that a local Legal Aid Committee will be unimpressed and decline to support, or alternatively in the belief that the claim being purely a 'try on', it will not be persisted in once firmness is shown. Disclosure in such cases may encourage the would-be plaintiff, and there can be few case notes of the 'chronic' hospital patient which, when viewed with hindsight, could not give some grounds, however insubstantial, on which anyone so minded could seek to build a case and pursue it in the hope of a nuisance value settlement. The reverse of the coin is where it is thought that the patient or his advisers genuinely believe that they have a case, but that belief is founded on error. It might well seem to a layman that if a patient is discharged from a hospital and dies within a short period thereafter, someone must have been negligent. This is, however, as every doctor knows, very far from being the case, and in such circumstances an offer to disclose the notes to any doctor nominated by the patient's relatives or their legal adviser will sometimes make it clear that either the condition from which the patient was suffering could not have been diagnosed or that even if it had been, death could not have been avoided.

However, an application can be made under the Supreme Court Act 1981 for disclosure of documents before the commencement of proceedings, providing the person making the application is likely to be a party to subsequent proceedings, that a claim is likely to be made in respect of personal injury or in respect of a person's death, that the person against whom the order is sought is likely to be a party to such proceedings, and that such person has or is likely to have any relevant documents in his possession, custody or power.

It may therefore be deemed imprudent to refuse a request for disclosure except in cases where it appears there is a try-on, and solicitors may think twice before advising their clients to incur the cost of making application to the Court for disclosure.

An application may also be made for an order for the disclosure of documents by a person who is not a party to existing proceedings. Therefore a general practitioner or surgeon can be required to supply records of a patient if the Court is satisfied that the records are relevant to an issue arising out of the proceedings. Prior to application being made to the Court a request for the records will be made by the solicitor in, for example, motor accident and employer's liability claims. Providing that the doctor receives a signed form of consent for release from his patient, there is little point in withholding the documents requested.

Summons for Directions

A Summons for Directions is sought to ensure that orders may be given regarding the conduct of the case to achieve the minimum of delay and of costs. In order to speed up the process there are now automatic

Directions which are applicable in some personal injury actions. Automatic Directions deal with interlocutory matters such as exchange of medical and experts' reports. If a Summons is taken out this will come before a Master, and applications may be made for an order against the other party should he fail to comply with the automatic Directions and/or to deal with other Directions such as amendment of pleadings or transfer to the County Court. A party may apply to the Court for an order that the opposing party should submit further and better particulars of the pleadings on the basis that those submitted are inadequate or ambiguous. Either party may apply for leave to serve Interrogatories, that is questions which must be answered on oath by means of swearing an affidavit. Admission of affidavit and documentary evidence and the number of expert witnesses permitted by each side will also be dealt with by the Master in the event that agreement is not reached between the parties.

Setting Down for Trial

Under the automatic Directions the action should be set down within six months of the close of pleadings in personal injury claims. Alternatively, on a Summons for Directions, the Master will make an order that the matter should be set down within a stated period, in the appropriate list. Application may be made by either party for a date for the trial to be fixed, and should no application be made, the action remains in the general list and moves into what is known as the Warned List, following which it may be heard at less than 24 hours' notice.

Trial

In a civil case it is sufficient for a plaintiff to prove his case on the balance of probability, whereas in a criminal trial a Judge or jury where applicable must be satisfied beyond all reasonable doubt of the defendant's guilt. The party on whom the burden lies, that is the task of establishing the facts necessary for the case to succeed, has the right to begin, and the first speech is therefore that of the Counsel for such party opening the case. The pleadings will make it clear where the burden of proof lies. In the simplest action the plaintiff affirms and the defendant defends and the burden of proof therefore lies on the plaintiff. In the event of the burden of proof of all the issues in the action lying on the defendant, the defendant's Counsel will open the case.

Following Counsel's opening speech he examines his witnesses. They are subsequently cross-examined by Counsel for the opposite party who attempts to discredit or minimise the implications of the evidence, and then re-examined with a view to re-establishing or clarifying the points on which the cross-examination may have cast doubt.

Counsel for the opposing party then opens his case and his witnesses are in turn examined, cross-examined, and re-examined. He then sums up and the final speech is by Counsel for the opening party. In the event of the opposing party not producing any witnesses, however, Counsel for the opposing party has the right to the final speech, a right which is greatly valued and which may lead to a decision not to use a witness and, rather than have the value of his testimony, have the right to the last word.

Depending upon whether or not there is a jury, the Judge will either deliver judgment or sum up and instruct the jury as to the law. The jury, when present, have the duty of determining the facts, and following consideration, will find for one or other party and decide on the quantity of damages. Juries sit in civil cases nowadays only rarely, but at the discretion of the Court may be used in cases such as defamation and malicious prosecution.

Judgment

Judgments, following the trial, are entered either at the central office of the Royal Courts of Justice or at the District Registry.

Execution

The successful party following judgment may obtain a Writ of Execution, and if the judgment is not satisfied it is open to him to take various proceedings depending upon the judgment debtor's assets and liabilities, and the latter may in certain cases apply for Stay of Execution.

Taxation of Costs

Costs, though usually following the event, that is, being awarded to the successful party, are at the discretion of the Court, and are assessed by the Taxing Master or District Registrar. High Court costs are appreciably greater than those of the County Court, and one who uses the High Court when the County Court would have been appropriate may find himself penalised in that only County Court costs may be allowed. An order is made at the trial for the costs to be taxed if not agreed between the parties.

Appeal Procedure

An appeal from the County Court or from the Queen's Bench Division is made to the Court of Appeal by Notice of Motion stating the grounds on which the appeal is based. The appellant may seek a reversal of the decision of the lower court, grounding his case on questions of fact or of law, or alternatively may seek a new trial of the action.

The Court of Appeal has authority to make or vary any order or to award any judgment that the case may require. Should it appear to the Court that evidence was incorrectly admitted or excluded in the lower Court, or that damages were assessed on incorrect principles, a new trial may be ordered. Alleged excessive damages are seldom grounds for a new trial, and it is, in general, necessary to show not only that evidence was improperly excluded or admitted, but that a material miscarriage of justice has likely resulted from such error.

From the Court of Appeal, appeal lies to the House of Lords, but this may only be pursued with the leave of either the Court of Appeal or of the House of Lords. Direct appeal from the High Court to the House of Lords, known as the leapfrog procedure, is possible under strictly defined circumstances and must concern a point of law of public importance.

European Court of Justice

If a case that comes before the County Court or the High Court concerns interpretation of EEC Acts or of the Treaty of Rome, the Court may refer the matter to the European Court provided that the ruling is necessary and concerns a difficult and important point.

Procedure in Criminal Courts

Information, Summons, and Warrant

Criminal procedure commences by information being laid before a Magistrate that an offence has been committed, and the Magistrate issuing a Summons or Warrant. A Summons is a document outlining the charge and ordering the accused to whom it is addressed to appear to answer it. A Warrant is a document stating the offence and the offender, addressed to the police, ordering that the offender be brought before the Magistrate, i.e. it is an authorisation of arrest.

The accused may be tried summarily, i.e. at a Magistrate's Court, or on indictment, i.e. before a jury at a Crown Court, the best known in London being the Central Criminal Court commonly known as the Old Bailey.

Magistrates' Courts

Magistrates' Courts are presided over largely by lay Magistrates, known as Justices of the Peace, advised by qualified clerks, but in London and some of the larger cities, paid stipendiary Magistrates sit, and they are barristers or solicitors of not less than seven years' standing. The Magistrates are addressed as 'Sir' or 'Madam', and less commonly today as 'Your Worship'.

Crimes can be divided initially between summary offences, tried before Magistrates without a jury, and indictable offences, tried in the Crown Court with a jury after a preliminary hearing in the Magistrate's Court.

Certain offences can only be tried summarily, such as most road traffic offences. Other offences are triable either way. Finally there are offences triable only on indictment, for example murder. In the case of an offence being triable either way, a Magistrate, after hearing representation as to the mode of trial from each side, decides if the case should be tried summarily, subject to the consent of the accused.

Summary Trial Procedure

The charge is read to the accused, who is asked whether he pleads guilty or not guilty. If he pleads guilty the facts of the case are given by the prosecution and the police will give evidence regarding past offences and character. A plea in mitigation of sentence may then be made on behalf of the accused, following which sentence is passed.

In the case of certain minor offences the accused may plead guilty by post and can submit a written statement in mitigation which will be considered by the Magistrate prior to sentence being passed.

Should the plea be 'not guilty', the prosecutor makes an opening address and witnesses for the prosecution are then examined, cross-examined and re-examined. At the end of the case for the prosecution it may be submitted on the accused's behalf that there is no case to answer, and should this plea be upheld the charge is dismissed. The accused may make an unsworn statement from the dock, remain silent, or more commonly give evidence and be cross-examined, and witnesses for the defence are then heard in like sequence.

If the defence produces evidence which the prosecution may not have foreseen, the Court may permit rebuttal evidence to be called by the prosecution. This occurs only in very exceptional cases.

Following completion of the evidence, the defence addresses the Court. The Magistrates then acquit or convict the accused, and following conviction the prosecution will submit to the Court details of any previous convictions. These details are given by a police officer, and the defence has a right to cross-examine the police officer concerning the previous convictions and the defendant's character generally. The accused or his representative then has the right to make a 'plea in mitigation' before sentence is passed. In general, imprisonment awarded by Magistrates may not exceed six months, though where two or more indictable offences dealt with summarily are involved, the total sentence may be up to twelve months.

Apart from awarding imprisonment and fines, the Magistrates may, following conviction, put the offender on probation, give him an absolute or conditional discharge, a suspended sentence of imprisonment, or make an order that he be bound over to keep the peace and be of good behaviour or carry out community service. A probation order puts the offender under the care of a probation officer for a period from six months to three years and may impose conditions, breach of which will render him liable to punishment. Where a conditional discharge is given the offender becomes liable to punishment, both for the further offence and the offence of which he has been convicted, should he commit another offence within a specified period. Provided he has no further conviction during that period the case is closed. The effect of an order upon a person to be bound over to keep the peace and be of good behaviour is that the offender is required to enter into a recognisance, with or without sureties, and if he fails to abide by the order during the period stated, he stands to forfeit the recognisance. It is not necessary to show that a further offence has been committed to prove a breach of the order. Where Magistrates are trying summarily an offence which could be tried on indictment, and having had details as to the accused's character and antecedents, consider that a sentence beyond their power to award is indicated, the case may be referred to the Crown Court for sentence.

Committal Proceedings

If the offence is an indictable one, or if the accused has elected trial on indictment, the Magistrates proceed as examining Justices, the hearing being known as a 'committal'. It is not in these circumstances for the Magistrates to decide the accused's guilt but to consider if there is sufficient evidence to commit the accused to stand trial at the Crown Court. The prosecution therefore has to show that there is a *prima facie* case against the accused.

The normal procedure is that all the evidence consists of written statements, and the examining Justices, if satisfied that there are adequate grounds, commit the accused for trial at the Crown Court. This can be done providing the accused does not object to any statement, does not wish to give evidence or call witnesses and does not wish to submit that there is insufficient evidence for a committal.

Alternatively, the accused may wish to challenge the prosecution's evidence in the hope that the examining Justices will decide that there is insufficient evidence to commit him for trial or, alternatively, no case to answer. In this situation there may be a formal hearing with the prosecution witnesses giving their evidence and then being cross-examined by the defence, or if the accused accepts the prosecution's statements, they may be read out to the Court, and then the accused's legal representative will submit that the evidence is such that the accused should not be committed for trial. The Magistrates then either dismiss the charge or, considering that there is a *prima facie* case, commit the accused for trial at the Crown Court.

Procedure at the Crown Court

England and Wales are divided into circuits and each circuit has a number of towns designated at different tiers. The first tier centred in the larger towns hears the more serious criminal cases.

There are three different classes of Judges sitting at the Crown Court: High Court Judges who are normally Judges of the Queen's Bench Division, Circuit Judges, and Recorders. Circuit Judges, who can also sit as County Court Judges, are appointed from barristers of at least ten years' standing and from Recorders of at least five years' standing. Recorders are barristers or solicitors of at least ten years' standing who act as part-time Judges.

Offences are divided into four classes. Class One offences, such as murder, are always tried by a High Court Judge. Class Two offences, such as manslaughter, rape, incest, infanticide, abortion and child destruction, are usually tried by a High Court Judge, but may be released by the presiding Judge to a Circuit Judge or Recorder. Offences of class Three and Four, being less serious, may be heard by a High Court Judge, Circuit Judge or Recorder. Justices of the Peace sit with a Judge when a Crown Court is hearing an appeal from a Magistrate's Court or proceedings on committal for sentence.

The accused having been arraigned, that is to say, the formal charge having been read to him, he is asked to plead. Apart from pleading guilty or not guilty, there are a number of other possibilities. The accused may, subject to the discretion of the prosecution and the Court, plead guilty to a lesser offence than that charged, and if this plea is accepted, the Court will proceed as though he had been charged only with the lesser offence. He may stand mute, when a jury will have to decide whether he does so of malice, or by visitation of God. If the former, a plea of not guilty is entered, and if the latter, a jury is charged to say whether or not the defendant is under a disability so that he cannot be tried. This will not be the same jury who may then determine his guilt or innocence. An accused may plead to the jurisdiction of the Court, that is to say that the Court has no right to try him; demur, that is put forward that the facts alleged and admitted do not constitute the offence charged; or plead that he has previously been pardoned, acquitted or convicted in respect of the same offence.

Where the accused pleads guilty, the prosecutor states the facts of the case and the police report on his character and previous offences. Any character witnesses for the accused are then heard, a plea in mitigation may be made and sentence is passed.

Where the plea is not guilty, the prosecutor opens his case, his witnesses are examined, cross-examined and re-examined. The defence has an opening speech only if he is calling witnesses as to the facts. If only the accused is being called with character or alibi witnesses, there is no opening speech. The accused on being called to give evidence on oath will be subjected to cross-examination by the prosecution. The accused does not have to give evidence and can remain silent or provide an unsworn statement from the dock, in which case he will not be cross-examined.

The defence witnesses may then be called, be examined, cross-examined and re-examined. Following conclusion of the evidence, Counsel for each side are entitled to address the jury, the prosecution always being heard first so that the defence has the last word.

The Judge then sums up and explains the law on the points at issue. The jury have the duty of deciding the facts of the case and returning their verdict. Apart from finding the accused guilty or not guilty, they may find him guilty of a lesser offence in certain circumstances; guilty on some counts of the indictment and not guilty on others; guilty of the attempt in certain circumstances; or not guilty by reason of insanity if the issue has been raised. If the jury cannot reach a unanimous verdict after a minimum of two and a quarter hours, the Judge may direct the jury that he can accept the majority verdict provided at least ten are agreed, or nine if there are only ten jurors.

Where the accused has been found guilty, the prosecution informs the Court of his previous convictions and character, a plea in mitigation may be made and sentence is passed.

Sentences of imprisonment and fines need no comment here. Probation, absolute and conditional discharge, and binding over have been referred to in the section dealing with Magistrates' Courts. The accused in either Court can admit to other offences and, at his request, and at the discretion of the trial Judge these can be taken into consideration in the determination of the sentence. Irrespective, however, of the number of offences taken into consideration, the sentence passed may not exceed the maximum provided for the offence of which the accused has been convicted.

A person found not guilty by reason of insanity, a verdict introduced by the Criminal Procedure (Insanity) Act 1964, may be detained during Her Majesty's Pleasure, and such a detention may be in a 'special hospital' if it be considered that maximum security is indicated. There is provision for an appeal against the finding of 'not guilty by reason of insanity'.

Either the Magistrates or the Crown Court may also, when a convicted offender is suffering from mental illness, psychopathic disorder, subnormality, or severe subnormality of a nature or degree which warrants detention for treatment, make an order for compulsory admission to a mental hospital, under Section 60 of the Mental Health Act 1959. It is necessary for such an order that two doctors, one being a psychiatrist, certify the above information, that a hospital can accept the offender within 28 days, and that the Court considers such admission to be the best method of dealing with the case. The order lapses after a period of 12 months but can be renewed.

If it is felt that the offender is violent or dangerous, he may be detained at a special hospital, and in this situation a restriction order can be made by the Crown Court under Section 65 of the Act.

The Powers of Criminal Courts Act 1973 enables any court to require that an offender on probation be submitted for treatment for a specified period not exceeding 12 months, providing evidence is given by a doctor, approved under the Mental Health Act, that this may improve his mental condition.

Appeal Procedure

From a Magistrate's Court the accused may appeal to the Crown Court against sentence if he pleaded guilty, and against conviction and sentence should he have pleaded otherwise. The appeal in the case of an appeal against conviction amounts to a re-hearing of the case, and will be heard by a Circuit Judge or Recorder sitting with Magistrates. The Appeal Court has the power to allow or dismiss the appeal, or may vary the Magistrates' decision. The sentence passed may be increased, though not beyond the maximum which the Magistrate's Court could have imposed for the particular offence.

Apart from an appeal to the Crown Court which is open only to the accused, either party may take the case to the Queen's Bench Division by asking the Magistrates to state a case. This procedure is used where a point of law is involved, and the Divisional Court may confirm the Magistrates' decision or return the case to them with directions to convict or acquit. The Queen's Bench Division may also, by an Order of Certiorari, consider the decisions of an inferior court and quash them either for want of jurisdiction or for a defect appearing on the face of the record.

From the Crown Court appeal lies to the Criminal Divison of the Court of Appeal and, again, this appeal may be against sentence or against conviction. Appeal may also be made to the Queen's Bench Division by way of case stated, and this procedure is open to either party.

Beyond the Criminal Division of the Court of Appeal lies the House of Lords, whence a case may be taken only on the certificate of the Court of Appeal or House of Lords to the effect that the case involves a point of law of particular importance, and that it is desirable in the public interest that the matter should be further appealed.

The Medical Witness

A practitioner must attend Court if he receives a subpoena or Summons. In a civil case the subpoena must be accompanied by conduct money, i.e. money to cover the cost of attendance at Court.

Few doctors enjoy attending court as a witness. Doctors are more used to asking questions than to answering them; they may feel that they have divided loyalties as when the custody of children is being contested and both husband and wife are the doctor's patients; and they resent the waste of time so often involved. When asked to appear, however, they might reflect that justice depends upon the willingness of the citizen to assist the courts and that this public duty applies particularly to those who, because of their specialist training and experience, are more likely than the average citizen to be objective and unbiased in their observations and recollections.

Having then agreed to attend Court, the doctor should prepare himself by reading the relevant case notes, etc., refresh his memory by reference to text books and recent papers on the subject, and, wherever possible, have a preliminary discussion with Counsel or solicitors so as to be prepared for the questions with which he is likely to be faced. The border between the expert witness and the witness of fact is a thin one, and the latter cannot reasonably object to being asked an opinion on matters within the knowledge of every doctor. He should, however, have made his limitations as an expert clear to the solicitor calling him well before the trial, and indicated if he felt that a doctor of greater or different experience should be called, stressing if need be that as a witness of fact he would refuse to enter into the realm of expert opinion.

When giving evidence, the doctor must avoid giving the impression that he is deciding the issue or that he is biased in favour of the party calling him. He should regard his function as that of assisting the Court to come to a decision, and should admit without hesitation facts which tend to favour the opposite party. It is seldom indeed that every fact points in the one direction, and the doctor who admits that there is something to be said for the other side will carry far more conviction than he who appears as an active protagonist.

How well the doctor stands up to cross-examination will largely depend upon how well his original observations were made, and how well he has done his homework before attending Court. Perhaps seldom can a more inauspicious start have been made than when the writer returned home in the early hours of one morning after an emergency call to find that the telephone exchange had rung to say that the gale which was raging had put another doctor's telephone line out of action and that they had an emergency call for him. No particulars of the case were given, and on arriving at the cottage in a nearby village, I was escorted into the parlour by the patient's wife and prior to sitting down removed with my ungloved hand the broken stock of a rifle which was on the armchair. This was to prove to be the murder weapon.

Having then decided how far he can go, for in medical matters there is seldom complete certainty, the doctor should choose his words with care, and with equal care see that they be not twisted, exaggerated, or belittled. He may admit other possibilities, and to say 'it is possible but it is not my opinion' can be a very telling reply. His answers should, wherever possible, be couched in simple terms, ignorance is usually better admitted immediately—it is difficult to ask many more questions once a witness has said that he does not know the answer—and, most important of all, a doctor should not go outside his field of expertise or experience. A houseman apeing a consultant, or a pathologist airing his clinical opinion, will seldom for long escape censure.

Medical Privilege

The medical witness can claim no privilege in Court in respect of information he has obtained in the course of his professional work. The law, which might punish a doctor who acts in breach of the implied contract of professional secrecy, also requires such a breach when a doctor appears to give evidence. While there have been isolated instances of doctors declining to reply to questions involving knowledge gained in professional consultation—one case concerned the secrecy required by VD regulations, and in another a psychiatrist's refusal to disclose confidential information was upheld by the Court—in general this course cannot be recommended. It is perfectly proper to point out to the Court that the information was obtained under circumstances of professional secrecy and to ask whether the question need be answered. Provided, however, that the point is a relevant one, the doctor will be told that he must answer, and should he refuse, will stand in contempt of Court and be liable to imprisonment.

The advisability of granting professional privilege to doctors is a thorny question. In some cases the ends of justice might be thwarted; in others needless harm to the individual's reputation would be avoided. The thought of the doctor being required to disclose in Court such information as he may receive in the consulting room doubtless influences very few patients when they seek a consultation, but in the case of these few, potential harm exists. There is no easy answer and it is doubtful if anything as clumsy as legislation could improve the present position. Perhaps in the last resort it lies with the judiciary to endeavour to balance the needs of justice with the general good of the public in each case where the problem arises.

Legal Aid

The provision of Legal Aid for civil proceedings is now contained in the Legal Aid Act 1974 and Legal Aid (General) Regulations 1980. They provide that persons whose disposable capital and income are below a specified limit will be awarded all or part of their costs in the majority of types of civil actions. An applicant has to prove to the local Legal Aid Committee that he has reasonable grounds for bringing or defending the case, but so far as actions in negligence against doctors are concerned this hurdle does not appear to be a high one. In the event that an assisted plaintiff loses the action the successful defendant can be awarded costs out of the Legal Aid Fund, but this is only done where the Court is satisfied that it is just and equitable, that the proceedings were instituted by the person receiving Legal Aid, and that the Court considers that the unassisted person will suffer severe financial hardship unless the award is made. These provisions result in many cases being settled quite irrespective of their merits, for where settlement can be achieved for an amount not materially greater than the defence would cost and the plaintiff is legally aided, it must then frequently be in the defendant's interest to settle.

Understandably the situation appears unfair to unassisted defendants, and many defendants' representatives may feel that it would have been more appropriate for the legislature to have given a successful defendant a right to claim costs subject to the Court's overriding discretion.

9 Professional Ethics

It may be useful first to define the interest which four bodies, the General Medical Council, the World Medical Association, the British Medical Association, and the protection organisations, have in matters ethical.

The General Medical Council

Until the coming into effect of the Medical Act 1978, the GMC had a limited interest, for its disciplinary jurisdiction was confined to considering cases where a doctor had been convicted by the courts, or where the action complained of could, if proved, amount to serious professional misconduct. The Act, however, permits the Council to provide advice for the profession on matters of professional conduct or ethics. The extent to which use will be made of this power remains, at the time of writing, to be seen.

The World Medical Association

The WMA, shortly after its formation in 1947, prompted to a large extent by the fact that a not insignificant number of doctors in Germany had prostituted their profession to the whims of a political maniac, drew up a modern version of the Hippocratic Oath—the Declaration of Geneva—in the hope that whatever politicians might do in the future, there would throughout the world be one class of men and women whose ideals of service would remain above any consideration of race, religion, colour or creed.

The Declaration states:

> At the time of being admitted as a Member of the Medical Profession

I solemnly pledge myself to consecrate my life to the service of humanity.

I will give to my teachers the respect and gratitude which is their due;

I will practise my profession with conscience and dignity;

I will respect the secrets which are confided in me;

I will maintain by all means in my power the honour and the noble traditions of the medical profession;

My colleagues will be my brothers;

I will not permit considerations of religion, nationality, race, party politics, or social standing to intervene between my duty and my patient;

I will maintain the utmost respect for human life from the time of conception; even under threat, I will not use my medical knowledge contrary to the laws of humanity.

I make these promises solemnly; freely, and upon my honour.

From the Declaration, the World Medical Association derived an International Code of Medical Ethics to which mankind must hope that members of, and all who aspire to membership of, the brotherhood of medicine will at all times subscribe. The code sets out the duties of doctors as follows:

Duties of Doctors in General

A doctor must always maintain the highest standards of professional conduct. A doctor must practise his profession uninfluenced by motives of profit.

The following practices are deemed unethical:

1 Any self advertisement except such as is expressly authorised by the National Code of Medical Ethics.
2 Collaboration in any form of medical service in which the doctor does not have professional independence.
3 Receiving any money in connection with services rendered to a patient other than a proper professional fee, even with the knowledge of the patient.

Any act or advice which could weaken the physical or mental resistance of a human being may be used only in his interest.

A doctor is advised to use great caution in divulging discoveries or new techniques of treatment.

A doctor should certify or testify only to that which he has personally verified.

Duties of Doctors to the Sick

A doctor must always bear in mind the obligations of preserving human life.

A doctor owes to his patient complete loyalty and all the resources of his science. Whenever an examination or treatment is beyond his capacity he should summon another doctor who has the necessary ability.

A doctor shall preserve absolute secrecy on all he knows about his patient, because of the confidence entrusted in him.

A doctor must give emergency care as a humanitarian duty, unless he is assured that others are willing and able to give such care.

Duties of Doctors to Each Other

A doctor ought to behave to his colleagues as he would have them behave to him.

A doctor must not entice patients from his colleagues.

A doctor must observe the principles of 'The Declaration of Geneva' approved by the WMA.

The WMA has subsequently made Declarations on major ethical issues as in the Declarations of Helsinki, Sydney, Oslo and Tokyo, reproduced in Appendix A.

The British Medical Association

The interest of the BMA is a wide one and includes all ethical problems arising between members of the Association. It will also act when only one of the doctors concerned is a member, provided that the other or others agree to accept the findings of the Ethical Committee.

The Central Ethical Committee is a standing committee of the Council of the BMA, and Ethical Committees are appointed by the divisions of the Association. Where one member feels that he has grounds for complaint against another, he is required by the Ethical Rules to put his complaint in writing and invite the respondent practitioner's comments, at the same time informing him that consideration is being given to invoking the ethical machinery. The correspondence is then submitted to the Secretary of the Local Ethical Committee who seeks advice regarding the action to be taken, from the headquarters of the Association.

The BMA being a voluntary association with the inevitable strengths and weaknesses of such bodies, cannot of course take any measures against a doctor comparable to those within the power of the GMC. The most serious steps open to the BMA are to expel a doctor from membership and to publicise among the profession its condemnation of his actions. Because of this relative impotency, it is in some circles fashionable to decry the BMA and to consider its ethical machinery as being without value. This view is thought to be based on a misconception of the whole purpose of ethical machinery.

If it can be agreed that the medical profession must needs maintain a high moral and ethical standard, it follows that it must be the duty of some body to lay down what is and what is not acceptable in ethical matters, and to consider and adjudicate upon cases brought to its notice. The profession would doubtless prefer that such authority should come from within rather than be imposed upon it from without. The BMA is the only association with the membership and organisation which entitles it to speak for the profession as a whole. Whatever then may be the individual's view of the BMA's position in medico-political and other spheres, and even if one considers that one's own sectional interest is better catered for by some other organisation, yet the maintenance of the ethical standards of the profession depends to a material extent upon the support the individual member of the profession is prepared to give to his national association. The BMA may be a self-appointed arbiter of the profession's ethics, but its position as such is unchallenged and the profession as a whole, members and non-members alike, have reason to be grateful for its services in this respect.

It has been said that the view that the lack of power to impose severe penalties makes the ethical machinery largely valueless is based on a misconception. The vast majority of ethical problems which arise are not matters that require a severe penalty, and the prime object of the ethical machinery is not to punish but to conciliate. Most troubles commence as little ones—misunderstanding, lack of tact, pique, fit of temper, a letter written in the heat of the moment—all these add fuel to the fire, and any apportioning of blame which may be required is very secondary to the re-establishment of normal intra-professional relations.

The BMA publishes the *Handbook of Medical Ethics*, which deals in some detail with the doctors' relationships with the State, groups in society, the media, and individuals, patients and others.

Protection Organisations

The protection societies are the fourth type of organisation with an interest in ethical matters, and their services in this respect are threefold. First, doctors will often approach their society for advice. It is to everyone's advantage if advice is sought as soon as the danger signal is sighted. Advice may then be prophylactic rather than therapeutic. Direct advice may be all that is required, but where two doctors are in conflict they will often be prepared to accept a suggestion that the points at issue be considered by one or more members of the professional secretariat of their society, or between members of the secretariat of their respective societies, and an amicable settlement can usually be achieved.

When more involved matters are concerned, and particularly where legal or quasi-legal points are involved, the protection society may be prepared to arrange arbitration provided that all parties to the dispute agree to accept the arbitrator's decision as final and binding.

Third, and fortunately infrequently in ethical matters, a protection society may be prepared to support its members by undertaking legal proceedings.

Such a case occurred when a practitioner sought, via legal channels, to prevent the hearing of a complaint against him by the Central Ethical Committee of the BMA. The circumstances were that Dr A, an ophthalmic medical practitioner, practised in partnership with Dr B, who decided to leave the partnership with a view to seeking further training and experience in the hope of obtaining a consultant appointment. It was agreed that Dr B might return to the partnership later, but meanwhile Dr C was engaged as a locum tenens. After a period of time Dr B announced that he would not be returning and Dr C continued to function as before. Subsequently, however, Dr A discovered that Dr C had, without reference to him, agreed to accept employment in a local NOTB centre being set up by a firm of dispensing opticians. Dr A thereupon terminated his association with Dr C and lodged a complaint through the BMA Ethical Committee.

Dr A was then surprised to receive a letter from Dr C's solicitors notifying him that Dr C was considering initiating legal action against him, whereupon Dr A sought the advice of his protection organisation. He was informed that no possible grounds for such action could be discerned, and that it seemed that this was probably intended as a delaying tactic to hold up any ethical enquiry. The BMA were informed of this view but, nevertheless, the Central Ethical Committee postponed action.

After some months had elapsed without legal proceedings being initiated, the Central Ethical Committee again aranged a hearing. Dr C changed solicitors and again threatened legal action, and despite the protest of the protection organisation, the Central Ethical Committee again postponed their proposed investigation. When, after a further lapse of months, a date was again fixed for the hearing, Dr C, having meanwhile returned to his original solicitors, issued a Writ two days before the date arranged for the hearing; again the society urged the BMA to proceed but once more the hearing was postponed. No Statement of Claim followed the Writ until the society's solicitors informed Dr C's solicitors that unless a Statement was delivered within seven days it was intended to issue a Summons to dismiss the action for want of prosecution. The Statement of Claim then produced sought declarations that the defendant had given his consent to the plaintiff undertaking consultative work under the Supplementary Ophthalmic Service, and that in undertaking such work the plaintiff was not acting contrary to ethics as set out in the BMA *Handbook*. The relevant paragraph was as follows:

> 'As a locum tenens is introduced in confidence to the practice of which he/she takes charge it must be presumed on principles of common equity that he cannot without dishonour commence practice in the neighbourhood where he has acted unless with a written consent obtained either from the practitioner whose substitute he has been or from the legal representatives of this practitioner.'

The Society's solicitors advised that no court would grant such declarations, for to do so would be to usurp the administrative function and discretion exercised by the Central Ethical Committee of the BMA. Counsel's opinion was then taken and this being to the effect that the Statement of Claim disclosed no cause of action, a

Summons was issued to strike out the Writ and Statement of Claim. This came before a registrar in a provincial District Registry who adjourned it for hearing by a Chancery Judge in London. The Judge determined that the relief sought by the plaintiff was in respect of an ethical matter and not in respect of any legal matters and ordered that the Writ and Statement of Claim be struck out and that Dr C's action be dismissed, Dr C to pay the costs. Leave to appeal was applied for and granted, but no appeal was lodged and further delay occurred in the time taken for the order striking out the Writ and Statement of Claim to be formally entered. Finally, more than two years after the original complaint, the matter was considered by the Central Ethical Committee, when it was resolved that Dr C had violated the generally accepted principles of professional conduct, in that he set up in independent practice in the area where he had acted as locum tenens, without taking adequate steps to satisfy himself that the consent of the partners to whom he had acted as locum tenens had been obtained, and that he be censured.

Common Ethical Problems

Intra-professional Relationships

A prominent medical jurist, when asked while giving evidence whether doctors were not generally agreed on a certain point, replied that he doubted whether there was any point on which doctors were generally agreed, an observation which brought forth from the Judge the heartfelt comment, 'You're telling me!' As it is in the nature of doctors to differ, it is essential for the patient's peace of mind that such differences are handled with tact and understanding. Unhappily, many students may have heard a consultant criticise a general practitioner's diagnosis and treatment. Such criticism, which often reflects the consultant's ignorance of general practice and professional ethics rather than any shortcomings on the part of the general practitioner, is the nadir of intra-professional relations.

Even should an error have occurred, provided the patient has not suffered material loss thereby, it is surely of paramount importance that the patient's confidence in her medical adviser should not be shaken. The writer has recollections, when in practice, of a baby being brought to his surgery on its way home from hospital where it had been for two or three days under observation following a head injury. The child's mother thought that one leg was not quite right, and on examination there was a fracture of the mid-shaft of the femur. How easy to criticise! What had the hospital been doing? On a moment's reflection, they had probably been doing exactly what the case demanded—watching for any sign indicative of rising intra-cranial pressure and meanwhile leaving the child resting peacefully in its cot. True, they had missed a fractured femur, but no harm had been done and the child had to be returned to the hospital for treatment of the fracture. The child's interest was that this return should not be attended by any implication of criticism. A word on the telephone, the child was returned, and no trouble ensued. Later the same week an elderly patient was seen who, having been in a road accident, had been taken to the casualty department of the same hospital and discharged home. He was complaining of pain in his hip and the external rotation of the leg made the diagnosis apparent on mere visual inspection. Had the casualty officer been negligent or had he seen a patient with an impacted fracture which might well have deceived anyone? What were my feelings towards that hospital after these events? The question is perhaps best answered by saying that various members of my family subsequently attended for treatment and I have sufficient humility to appreciate that the consultants, the registrars, and also the housemen of that hospital must, on occasion, have elicited signs which I had failed to discern though no word of any criticism having been expressed ever reached my ears.

The essence of intra-professional relations then is something more than common courtesy and consideration for one's professional colleagues, of whatever rank or whatever branch of the profession. It follows that the doctor must be at pains to avoid taking any unfair advantage of a colleague, and in no sphere is this more important than in the question of acceptance of patients.

The Representative Body of the BMA has recommended that a practitioner ought not to accept as his patient, save with the consent of the colleague concerned, the types of patient listed below.

1 Any patient or member of a patient's household whom he has previously attended, either as a consulting practitioner or as a deputy for a colleague.
2 Any patient or member of the patient's household whom he has attended within the previous two years in the capacity of assistant or locum tenens.
3 Any patient who at the time of the application is under active treatment by a colleague, unless he is personally satisfied that the

colleague concerned has been notified by the patient or his representatives that his services are no longer required.

4 Any patient who so applies because his regular medical attendant is temporarily unavailable. In such case he should render whatever treatment for the time being may be required, and should subsequently notify the patient's regular attendant of the steps he has taken.

A practitioner in whatever form of practice should take positive steps to satisfy himself that a patient who applied for treatment or advice is not already under the active care of another practitioner before he accepts him. If he is so satisfied he may accept him as his patient, but his acceptance should be subject to the considerations set out below.

A practitioner in any form of specialist practice should not, except in circumstances stated below, accept a patient for examination and advice except on a reference from a general practitioner or from another specialist, which should only be with the general practitioner's knowledge.

The specialist should ensure that the true position is ascertained at the time an appointment is booked, and should ask that an introductory letter be brought.

Exceptions:

1 Emergencies.
2 Where previous inquiry indicates that the consultation is for refraction examination only.
3 Consultations in venereology, either at clinics or in private.
4 Overseas visitors having no family doctor in the United Kingdom.
5 References from school or community health services with the knowledge of the general practitioner.
6 Consultations concerning contraception where a patient does not wish to consult her general practitioner.

After the consultation, where further medical care is indicated, and especially where such care is within the province of a general practitioner, the specialist should do all he can to persuade the patient to be referred to a general practitioner to whom a report and advice should be sent in the same way as if the consultation had arisen from a normal reference.

A general practitioner receiving such a report should be prepared to accept that the specialist is making a genuine attempt to establish the correct relationship between the patient and his doctor.

Examining Medical Officers

Circumstances not infrequently arise where a doctor is asked to examine another doctor's patient on behalf of a third party, such as an employer or insurance company. The examining doctor's report is sent to the party commissioning the examination and, in general, the doctor is not at liberty to inform the patient of his findings. During such examination information may be obtained of treatment the patient is receiving from his own doctor, and the examining doctor must take every care to avoid expressing criticism of such treatment. Where the examining doctor considers that the patient's future health requires him to communicate with the patient's own doctor, this he should do via or with the permission of the party commissioning the examination.

Under certain circumstances, and particularly where the examination is concerned with litigation, the patient's own doctor may be present and the examining doctor should be prepared to facilitate this. It goes without saying that an examining doctor must in no way attempt to persuade the person examined to become his patient.

Consultation

Before one has been many years in practice one becomes instinctively aware when a patient is likely to request a second opinion, and therefore one takes the initiative and recommends to the patient that a further opinion be obtained. So it is the young man who is faced with a patient demanding that he be referred to a specialist, and at whatever cost to one's pride, such a demand should very seldom be refused. This is not to say that the patient should be referred to the consultant of his choice, who might be entirely inappropriate, as in the case of a hypochondriac who, having arrived at the self-diagnosis that his heart strings were tied round his liver, consulted his general practitioner solely to enquire whether his condition necessitated the services of a cardiologist or a surgeon.

The patient having been referred to a consultant and his report having come to hand, the doctor must appreciate that he still retains complete responsibility for whatever treatment he may prescribe. It is no defence to an allegation of negligence nor to a charge of having prescribed a substance not considered by the NHS authorities to be a drug, to say that a consultant advised it. In the majority of cases a GP will follow a consultant's advice, but he must first satisfy himself that the advice is appropriate, and second, be prepared to accept responsibility for such treatment as he may order as a result of adopting the consultant's opinion. Where, rarely, the consultant's opinion is unacceptable and where such disagreement cannot be quickly resolved by direct contact, the patient must be told of the position which has arisen and be permitted to select one or other line of treatment or assisted to obtain a third opinion.

The domiciliary consultation perhaps provides the real test of both parties' understanding of the ethics of intra-professional relationship. Properly conducted the patient and his relatives should feel reassured not only regarding the patient's illness but also regarding his choice of practitioner. The consultant who cements the bonds between patient and practitioner will find his trouble well rewarded.

While it is highly desirable that assistants and partners should have a properly drawn up legal agreement, absence of this does not reduce the ethical duty which is owed by a partner, assistant, or locum to his ex-partner or principal, to refrain from any act which would damage his practice. Legal agreements usually have a barring out clause excluding the outgoing partner or assistant from practising within a stated radius for a stated time, but it is doubtful, in view of the case Hensman *v* Traill 1980*, whether such restriction would be upheld by the Court, and it is very possible that a ban on accepting patients of the former partner or principal would be considered all that could reasonably be required.

Be that as it may, the ethical duty remains, and unless a practitioner has the consent of his ex-partner or principal, preferably in writing, he should not set up in opposition. To determine whether an address at which a practitioner proposes to practise might be considered to amount to setting up in opposition, can be difficult, especially in urban areas. Advice on this point may be sought from local practitioners or from the BMA, and when any doubt at all exists, the outgoing partner, assistant, or locum is advised to inform the ex-partner or principal of his intention in writing, adding that he will take every care to avoid damaging his colleague's interest.

Relations with Other Professions

Dentists

It is undesirable that a doctor should appear to interfere in any way with a patient's free choice of dentist. When he is asked to recom-

* Hensman *v* Traill [1980] 124 SJ 776. *The Times*, 22 December.

mend a dentist it is preferable to name at least two and to take care that nothing said might be taken to denigrate others.

Following dental treatment, a complication having occurred, the patient will at times consult a doctor rather than return to the dentist, and the doctor should not take over the treatment without the dentist's consent. Usually the patient should be referred back to the dentist, but if for any reason this is not practicable every attempt should be made to contact the dentist and discuss the matter with him before treatment is initiated.

Where a dentist refers a patient to a doctor for an opinion or treatment of some inter-current medical condition, the doctor should be at pains to return the patient to the dentist as soon as appropriate, giving such information as the dentist may reasonably require to assist him in the future treatment of his patient.

When a dentist requires a general anaesthetic it is for him to choose the anaesthetist. If this is not the patient's own doctor, no objection should be raised to the doctor being present should this be desired.

Chemists

As in the case of dentists, it is undesirable that a doctor should refer patients to a specific chemist where a choice exists, and a doctor should not hold a financial interest in a chemist's business within the area of his practice. Whenever possible, a doctor should avoid sharing premises with a chemist—or with a dentist—as this might appear to militate against the exercise of the patient's free choice.

Professions Supplementary to Medicine and Paramedics

Chiropodists, dieticians, medical scientific officers, occupational therapists, orthoptists, physiotherapists, radiographers, and remedial gymnasts, are registered under the Professions Supplementary to Medicine Act 1960. They have their own ethical codes and disciplinary committees. It is perfectly proper therefore for a doctor to give members of these professions such information as is reasonably necessary for their full participation in the patient's diagnosis and treatment. The doctor maintains overall control of patients referred, and indeed only chiropodists may treat patients without medical referral.

Paramedics—under which term I include all unregistered groups—pose problems of confidentiality and competence. The doctor should endeavour to satisfy himself about the latter, and further should ensure that the patient accepts the paramedic's involvement and the passing of necessary information to him.

Relations with the Public

A practitioner should not sanction or acquiesce in anything which commends or directs attention to his professional skill, knowledge, services, or qualifications, or denigrates those of others, nor be associated with those who procure or sanction such advertising or publicity. It follows that every time a practitioner places or permits the placing of his name before the public he must be prepared to justify himself should it be alleged that his object was the promotion of his professional advantage.

Anonymity is therefore a powerful safeguard, but it is at the same time appreciated that there are occasions when it is proper for a doctor's name and perhaps his qualifications and position held to be mentioned. If a doctor in the popular press advises on the treatment of the common cold, it is clearly of no importance to the reader to know anything of the author beyond the fact that he is a doctor. Where, however, he is writing on a controversial matter in which the lay public have a legitimate interest and the subject is not one within the knowledge of every doctor, then the reader can reasonably require to know something of the author's standing so that he may judge with what authority he is putting forward his views.

It is clearly in the interests of the general public that one qualified by his experience to discuss the connection between smoking and carcinoma of the lung should be enabled to do so, and that the reader should be able to appreciate the full weight of authority which the writer commands. Such an article may, it is true, promote the author's professional advantage and the author must be prepared, if challenged, to show that this result was incidental and not a desired or sought after objective.

Therefore, when one is asked to write an article for the lay press or to lecture to a lay audience, it behoves one first to consider whether to permit one's name to be mentioned and, if this is thought desirable, then to minimise anything which might possibly be construed as advertising.

To this end neither name nor qualifications should be given undue prominence; there should be no laudatory comments in any introduction or prior notice of the article or lecture, and, most essential of all, the doctor should make it clear in writing to the editor of the publication or secretary of the organisation arranging the lecture that he is not prepared to accept any correspondence from would-be patients as a result of the publication or lecture. Further, he should be careful not to place his name before the public with undue frequency, nor do anything which might lead to his name becoming associated with any particular condition or form of treatment.

It is, unfortunately, a not uncommon experience for a doctor to give an interview to the press with all due care and circumspection, and subsequently to be appalled at what eventually appears in print. It is usually better to give a prepared statement rather than grant an interview or, alternatively, to seek an agreement that the proposed article will be submitted for approval before it is published. Even then, one may find one's statement misquoted so that the sense of it is totally altered, or that the promise to submit a proof is dishonoured. Regrettably, and to the detriment of the general public, many doctors after bitter experience conclude that the only thing to say to journalists is, 'no comment'.

Television and radio pose similar problems and the same principles apply. Where it is reasonably necessary for the practitioner's name to be given to demonstrate his authority on the subject, this is unobjectionable, but otherwise anonymity should be observed. No correspondence should be entered into or consultation granted to any viewer or listener. It goes without saying that a doctor should not be associated with any programme which has as its object the advertising of any medicine or surgical appliance.

Relations with Patients

Where a practitioner wishes to make some announcement to his patients, e.g. change of surgery hours or location, introduction of an appointment system, etc., he should do so by means of a sealed letter addressed only to such persons as he has reason to believe are his patients. Inevitably in a large practice, there will be some who are circularised and who are no longer patients of the practice, and any danger of being accused of advertising by writing to such persons can largely be avoided by a sentence along the lines, 'If by any chance you are no longer a patient of the practice kindly disregard this notice and accept my apologies'.

Occasions arise when a practitioner wishes to make a formal notification to his professional colleagues. A consultant or ophthalmic medical practitioner may be setting up in practice or changing his professional address, or a practitioner may wish to offer some service, perhaps ECG, to his colleagues. In all such cases a formal notice simply stating the essential facts should be sent, under cover, only to such practitioners as the sender has reason to believe would wish to receive it. Too wide a circulation gives a suggestion of advertising.

Notices at a practitioner's premises are external and internal. The former should be confined to the usual plate, unostentatious, and placed there to enable those seeking the doctor's premises to identify them and determine when the doctor may be consulted. Qualifications may appear but there should be no descriptive wording such as 'gynaecologist' or 'psychiatrist', though the phrase 'physician and surgeon' is perhaps hallowed by time. Notices inside the premises may be prominent, and here should be detailed matters such as times of clinics, times when each doctor is consulting, etc. As these notices are seen only by patients or potential patients of the practice, it is reasonable to give all such information as a patient might require and no question of advertising arises.

Patients also require to be able to find the doctor's name in the telephone directory, but this should appear only in ordinary small type. To put an entry in heavy type would draw attention to it and might well be construed as advertising. Local directories may cause trouble and the rule is that doctors' names may appear only in directories which purport to include the names of all practitioners in the locality, and that there should be no payment for the entry. Objection was taken to doctors' names appearing in a directory which was sold to them, and to all others whose names appeared, at a price higher than that at which it retailed. It was considered that the extra charge could only be a charge for the entry which thereby became an advertisement.

Medical Secrecy

The doctor/patient relationship is founded on professional confidence, the patient having the right to expect that his doctor will not disclose, without his patient's consent, information obtained during his professional attendance. The principle was reaffirmed by the General Assembly of the World Medical Association in 1973:

> 'Whereas: The privacy of the individual is highly prized in most societies and widely accepted as a civil right; and
>
> Whereas: The confidential nature of the patient–doctor relationship is regarded by most doctors as extremely important and is taken for granted by the patient; and
>
> Whereas: There is an increasing tendency towards an intrusion on medical secrecy;

Therefore be it resolved: That the 27th World Medical Assembly reaffirm the vital importance of maintaining medical secrecy not as a privilege for the doctor, but to protect the privacy of the individual as the basis for the confidential relation between the patient and his doctor; and ask the United Nations, representing the people of the world, to give to the medical profession the needed help and to show ways for securing this fundamental right for the individual human being.'

It is appreciated that in these days professional confidence is necessarily incomplete, the lack of privilege in Court and the notification of infectious diseases being particular examples. The doctor must, however, be on his guard to avoid giving confidential information to all manner of authorities, governmental, local, employing, police, inspectors of this and inspectors of that. The consent of his patient or of the patient's legal representative is necessary unless the patient's interest, the public interest, the law, or an approved research protocol requires an exception being made to the general rule.

Research on Children

Paediatrics cannot progress without research, yet there is doubt as to whether the common law permits parents or guardians to consent to any procedure being carried out on a child which is not for the child's personal benefit.

The British Paediatric Association in 1980 published 'Guidelines to aid Ethical Committees considering research involving children'.

These guidelines presume that four premises are accepted:

That research involving children is important for the benefit of all children and should be supported and encouraged and conducted in an ethical manner.

That research should never be done on children if the same investigation could be done on adults.

That research which involves a child and is of no benefit to that child (non-therapeutic research) is not necessarily either unethical or illegal.

That the degree of benefit resulting from a research should be assessed in relation to the risk, of disturbance, discomfort, or pain—the risk:benefit ratio.

Amplification of these guidelines will be found in Appendix B.

Clinical Trials

Trials of new drugs are officially sanctioned by the Committee on Safety of Medicines. The ethical aspects are controlled by the appropriate Ethical Committee within the hospital group. Doctors taking part in such trials should satisfy themselves that the principles of the Declaration of Helsinki are being observed and that the rights of the subjects of the trial are not being restricted by commercial or other interests: see Appendix A.

10 The General Practitioner in the National Health Service

Unlike hospital doctors, general practitioners are independent contractors. When a doctor applies to be included in the medical list of the Family Practitioner Committee, he signs a Form of Contract with that Committee which binds him to observe the 'Terms of Service for the time being in operation'. As the Secretary of State has the power to change, unilaterally, the terms of service, the doctor is, in effect, bound to observe such terms as the Minister may at any time introduce.

Whereas the hospital doctor (an employee of a health authority) is only liable to face disciplinary measures taken against him on three counts, personal conduct, professional conduct, and professional competence, in the case of the independent contractor, the general practitioner, it has been thought necessary to spell out in detail the offences which may lead him into conflict with the NHS authorities.

NHS Disciplinary Authorities

The general medical, general dental, pharmaceutical, and ophthalmic services are under the control of the Family Practitioner Committee. A Committee consists of laymen, doctors, dentists, chemists, and opticians, the professional members being elected by their local professional body—in the case of doctors, the Local Medical Committee. The Local Medical Committee itself is a body elected by and from the local general practitioners with representatives from the hospital and community health branches of the profession.

Medical Service Committees

Certain disciplinary matters come before the Local Medical Committee, but in addition, each Family Practitioner Committee has a Medical Service Committee which consists of a Chairman and six other persons, three of whom are appointed by and from the lay members of the Family Practitioner Committee and three by the Local Medical Committee. The Service Committee has the duty of considering complaints by or on behalf of patients and references from the Family Practitioner Committee relating to the administration of the Service.

A complaint by or on behalf of a patient against a doctor commences with a letter to the administrator of the Family Practitioner Committee. This is considered by the Chairman of the Service Committee, and if, usually first having sought the observations of the doctor, there is thought to be a *prima facie* case, the matter is considered at a hearing before the Service Committee. Paid legal representation is not permitted though the practitioner may be accompanied by a friend. Evidence is not taken on oath and the Committee subsequently reports to the Family Practitioner Committee stating whether it has found the practitioner to be in breach of his Terms of Service and if so what penalty is recommended. The possible penalties are a limitation of the doctor's list, a fine, or to use the Department's euphemism a 'withholding of remuneration', a caution, and representation to the Tribunal that the continued inclusion of the practitioner's name on the medical list would be prejudicial to the efficiency of the Service.

The Family Practitioner Committee almost invariably adopts the report of the Service Committee, and there is a right of appeal against the decision. A case fought on behalf of its member by the Medical Protection Society (Ellis *v* Ministry of Health, 1967) established the principle that the complainant may appeal only against a decision that a practitioner was not in breach of his terms of service and not against the penalty awarded when a breach has been found. The practitioner may not appeal against the reference to the Tribunal but may appeal against any other adverse decision, or may alternatively, where a financial penalty has been recommended, make representations, written or oral, against the amount of such fine.

The Secretary of State has the right to vary the recommendations of the Family Practitioner Committee giving, where appropriate, a further right of representations being made. Where an oral hearing of an appeal or representations takes place, legal representation is permitted and such appeal or representations are normally heard by three persons appointed by the Secretary of State, the Chairman usually being legally qualified, and at least one of those appointed being a medical practitioner. The persons hearing the appeal draw up a report to the Secretary of State, and finally, often after an interval of several months, the Secretary of State gives his decision.

The Tribunal, the body which has the duty of considering whether the continued inclusion of a practitioner's name in the medical list would be prejudicial to the efficiency of the Service, consists of the Chairman, who holds office during the pleasure of the Lord Chancellor, and a member appointed by the Secretary of State as representative of the Family Practitioner Committee. Doctors appearing before the Tribunal may be legally represented and there is provision for a subsequent appeal being made to the Secretary of State by the respondent practitioner.

Jurisdiction of Local Medical Committee

The Local Medical Committee is concerned with cases of alleged excessive prescribing, investigation of certification, record-keeping, fee charging and the determination of whether a substance prescribed was a drug. The regulations regarding these matters are quite unnecessarily complex and the drafting is the reverse of helpful. The net result is that matters in which there are other than medical interests, certification and record-keeping, are considered by a purely medical body, the Local Medical Committee, whereas entirely medical questions, excessive prescribing and the determination of whether a substance prescribed was a drug, are considered appropriate matters for a predominantly lay body, the Family Practitioner Committee, to advise upon.

Certification and Record-keeping

Where it appears to the Secretary of State that a practitioner has failed to carry out his obligations with regard to keeping clinical records of his patients or that he has failed to exercise reasonable care in the issue of Social Security Certificates, the matter is referred for consideration by the Local Medical Committee, the practitioner being entitled to submit a statement and/or appear before the Committee, a representative of the Secretary of State being similarly entitled to attend and be heard. The Committee draws up a report of its finding on the question of whether there has been a failure on the part of the practitioner, states its view of the extent and gravity of any such failure and may add a recommendation of what action, if any, should be taken by the Secretary of State. The practitioner has the right of appeal against an adverse finding and the Secretary of State, if dissatisfied, may refer the matter to referees for consideration. Finally, the Secretary of State determines whether to order a financial withholding, against which withholding the practitioner has the right to make representations, unless he has previously appealed.

Excessive Prescribing

Investigation of excessive prescribing commences with a reference by the Secretary of State to the Local Medical Committee, the practitioner having the choice of submitting a statement in writing or of appearing before the Committee, the Secretary's representative again having the right to be present when a hearing takes place. The Committee determines whether excessive cost has been incurred, estimates the excess and informs the Family Practitioner Committee, the practitioner, and the Secretary of State of its decision, having the right to add a statement of any considerations to which it feels the Family Practitioner Committee and the Secretary of State should have regard in making any recommendations or decision to withhold money. The practitioner has a right of appeal and the Secretary of State, if dissatisfied with the decision of the Committee, may refer the matter to referees. In any event, the case is subsequently reviewed by the Family Practitioner Committee whose duty it is to make recommendations to the Secretary of State with regard to any financial withholding. Where a financial withholding is imposed, the practitioner has the right to make representations unless he has previously appealed.

Whether a Drug

Whereas in hospital practice the doctor can prescribe what he considers his patient requires without further ado, the general practitioner must first consider whether the substance he proposes to prescribe is a drug or whether, in the particular circumstances, it would be considered to be a food or a cosmetic. It is therefore true to say that the general practitioner can prescribe whatever he decides his patients require, but to tell the whole truth one must add that the practitioner must be prepared to justify his prescription if challenged and to meet the cost himself should his prescription be disallowed. In particular, the general practitioner must not assume that a consultant's recommendation implies that the substance recommended is prescribable under the NHS, should avoid prescribing substances advertised to the public, and should realise that the powers that be have not the least hesitation in wasting hours of doctors' time over a matter of a few pounds.

The Secretary of State or the Family Practitioner Committee refer the question of whether a substance prescribed was a drug to the Local Medical Committee, and the practitioner may submit a statement in writing or appear before the Committee. Should the practitioner appear, representatives of the Department and of the Family Practitioner Committee have the right to be heard. The Committee reports its findings to the practitioner, the Family Practitioner Committee and the Secretary of State, and either of the first two may appeal to the Secretary of State; likewise the Secretary may refer the matter to referees should he be dissatisfied. Should it then be determined that the substance prescribed was not a drug which the Family Practitioner Committee was bound to supply, the estimated cost of the substance will be withheld from the practitioner's remuneration.

Fee Charging

With certain exceptions, questions of whether a fee can properly be charged are considered by the Local Medical Committee, and where the Committee and the Family Practitioner Committee disagree, or where they are agreed but the Secretary of State is dissatisfied with their decision, the matter goes for determination to referees whose decision is final.

Terms of Service

The Terms of Service which are set out in the National Health Service (General Medical and Pharmaceutical Services) Regulations 1974, Statutory Instrument 1974 No. 160 as amended by 1976 SIs Nos. 690 and 1407, first determine the types of persons for whose treatment a practitioner is responsible. Apart from those he has accepted or agreed to accept on his list or as temporary residents, there are persons to whom he has a duty under the Family Practitioner Committee's Allocation Scheme. The profession at the inception of the NHS agreed to accept responsibility for the entire population, so that no matter how selfish or irresponsible a patient's conduct may be he cannot be excluded from benefit. This necessitates a scheme whereby a patient who cannot find a doctor prepared to accept him can be allocated to a practitioner. In addition to being obliged to accept these patients, practitioners are also required to treat other doctors' patients in emergency where the patient's own doctor and his deputy are unavailable, and also to provide necessary treatment pending a patient being accepted by or allocated to a practitioner. A doctor has the right to have a patient removed from his list, though this, being subject to the restrictions of the Allocation Scheme, may prove impossible in rural and under-doctored areas.

The Terms of Service go on to categorise a practitioner's duty towards his patients. While many of these clauses might be thought to be self-evident, they are of importance in that it is the alleged breach of the letter of the Regulations which brings a matter before a Service Committee.

Other Regulations detail the practitioner's duty to provide accommodation, to issue certificates, to supply drugs where necessary, to keep records, to inform the Family Practitioner Committee of deputising arrangements and other administrative matters.

The Disciplinary Machinery in Practice

While the legislators draw up the Regulations, their working depends on the good sense or otherwise of the administrators, and in this context, primarily on the administrators of Family Practitioner Committees. There are some administrators who see their prime object as the smooth running of the Health Service in their area, and are quite prepared to pursue that goal without undue observation of the letter of the Regulations. Where a patient writes a letter which suggests that a misunderstanding has occurred, such an administrator will, rather than reach for the book of rules, apply his common sense and powers of conciliation, and in the majority of cases patient and practitioner will be reconciled. However, there are other administrators who will seek to make a case out of the least hint of discontent, and this approach to the problem is greatly assisted by a requirement in the Regulations that there be a hearing if 'the correspondence discloses a material difference between the parties with regard to the facts of the case'. The 'material difference' is often nothing more than a disagreement as to what was said on the telephone several weeks before, and this is sufficient to put the Service Committee procedure in motion. The results this achieves will be referred to later, but it is certain, whatever the formal result, that the rift between patient and practitioner will be widened. It is almost equally certain that the practitioner will become disenchanted with the National Health Service, and this procedure has been the final straw which has led more than one doctor to pack his bags and protest with his feet. The following cases are far from being unique.

A girl returned home from boarding school one day and her mother noted that she was thin and seemed unwell. The girl said that she had had a sore throat for which she had been under treatment for the preceding six weeks. The following day the mother went to work in the morning and remained at home with her daughter in the afternoon, but did not take her to see a doctor because of the inclement weather. On the morning of the next day, however, she phoned a doctor and asked that a visit should be paid. According to the doctor he visited the flat during the morning but was unable to obtain a reply, and did not think to leave a note saying that he had called. Shortly after commencement of evening surgery, the mother telephoned the surgery and spoke to the partner of the doctor she had requested to call. While there was some dispute regarding the details of the conversation, the doctor's contention was that he had not refused to visit but merely said that he could not come at that time and asked for a further call later if necessary. It was undisputed that the only symptom mentioned at this time was that of vomiting, for which the doctor gave advice. Nothing further was heard until the following morning when the doctor received an urgent message stating that the child was unconscious, whereupon he visited immediately and had the girl transferred to hospital. On the afternoon of that day the patient died, the cause of death being given as basal pneumonia and diabetic coma.

A complaint was lodged and the doctor's observations sought. He pointed out that the patient was not on his list, being on that of the school doctor, but added that this fact had in no way influenced his actions. The matter came to a hearing before the Service Committee when it was considered that the points requiring investigation were threefold. First, whether, if this was a case of emergency, the doctor had complied with his duty to give any necessary treatment as provided for by the Allocation Scheme; second, whether, if this was an emergency, the doctor had rendered whatever services were in the patient's best interest; and finally, whether, if the patient's condition so required, the doctor had visited and treated the patient.

Having heard both parties, the Committee came to the conclusion that, while it was the doctor's duty to attend the patient, the fact that her condition was a potentially serious one was not conveyed to the doctor. The Committee then, undeterred by its own observations, proceeded to find the doctor in breach of his terms of service in that he failed to visit and treat the patient whose condition so required, and also in that he failed to render all proper and necessary treatment.

An appeal was lodged on the doctor's behalf based on the contention that the doctor had no responsibility until, first, there existed an emergency, and second, the existence of such emergency was adequately conveyed to his notice. When asked for its views, the Family Practitioner Committee made the remarkable statement that, as at the time of the evening telephone call the child's condition was, in the Committee's opinion, potentially serious, it was bound to infer that the doctor had failed to render all proper and necessary treatment.

An oral hearing of the appeal ensued and in due course the decision was received, this being to the effect that the issue depended on the extent to which the doctor was made aware of the existence of any emergency, and finding that the urgency of the situation was not adequately conveyed to him, the appeal was allowed.

A Family Practitioner Committee received a lengthy communication signed by a retired Army officer, his wife, and a neighbour. This requested an investigation into the care and treatment given by a general practitioner to one of his patients, who was a neighbour but not a relative of any of the signatories of the letter. It was made quite apparent that it was the writers of the letter and not the patient who desired the inquiry. Among many complaints of neglect, failure to visit, failure to refer to hospital, inadequate treatment, etc., there was a statement to the effect that when the patient was admitted to hospital it was said that she would not otherwise have survived until the following morning. The administrator on receipt of this letter wrote to the secretary of the hospital seeking information regarding the patient's condition on admission, and informing him that the practitioner's conduct was the subject of investigation. The hospital secretary in reply forwarded a letter from the admitting medical officer giving briefly the diagnosis and the patient's general condition, adding that so far as the hospital was concerned the doctor had always been helpful and cooperative.

The doctor, being informed of the complaint, was advised by his protection society that he was not at liberty to disclose clinical details of his patient without her consent, and therefore as a first step he must ask the administrator for a copy of the authority he had doubtless obtained from the patient. The administrator replied that as the complaint was made by three neighbours of the patient who was herself incapable of making a complaint—an unsubstantiated assumption—the Chairman of the Medical Service Committee was of the opinion that the complaint should be investigated. What the administrator did not mention was that, on the day this letter was written, he also wrote to the patient seeking her authority for the proposed investigation. Written authority was given and a copy was received by the doctor four days before the Service Committee hearing. The time allowed obviously being inadequate to permit him to submit his observations, he requested a postponement which was refused but later granted on a direct approach by the protection society, which stressed the impossibility of the doctor giving his observations without infringing the code of professional secrecy, until such time as the patient's consent was obtained. The administrator was also informed that exception was taken to his statement that the complaint was made on the patient's behalf when it was clear that it was others who were seeking the investigation, and that it would have been expected in such a case that the patient's desires would have been ascertained initially on receipt of the complaint. A letter was then drafted for the doctor to send with his observations. This questioned *inter alia* the authority of the administrator to seek clinical information from the hospital secretary, an action which was challenged, first because these clinical details were sought without the patient's authority, and second because it accords ill with the impartial position a Family Practitioner Committee should occupy in these matters for it to seek evidence in support of one or other party to an inquiry. It was also pointed out that the patient was one of a problem family and had on no fewer than nine occasions taken her discharge from hospital against medical advice, and there was little difficulty in exposing the half-truths and demolishing the innuendoes with which the complainants' letter was liberally sprinkled. The postponed hearing before the Service Committee was then arranged for a date when the doctor had planned to be abroad on holiday and the Committee refused his application for postponement. The protection society protested that the first postponement was due to the Committee's handling of the matter. At this juncture the administrator received a letter from the patient asking that the case be dropped as it had been taken up without her request, and the papers she had signed had been produced when she was too ill to appreciate the situation. The social worker who forwarded the letter stated that the patient was most concerned that such accusations should have been made against her doctor.

A doctor having visited a child was asked to examine the father's ears. Having done so, he advised that olive oil be instilled for a few days and that the patient then attend his surgery for syringing. The next morning the patient attended the surgery and demanded a prescription for his ears. The doctor demurred, pointing out that only a few drops of olive oil were required, but the patient, being unwilling to accept this advice, announced his intention of changing his doctor. His medical card was signed and he then departed. A short while later the practitioner received from the administrator a copy of a letter of complaint from the patient, the allegations being that he had failed to provide all proper and necessary treatment and that he had failed to order on the form provided for the purpose such drugs and appliances as were requisite for the treatment of the patient. The doctor submitted his observations and was somewhat surprised, subsequently, to receive from the administrator a copy of a letter from the chairman of the Service Committee addressed to the administrator which contained the phrase, 'In my opinion there has been a breach of the doctor's Terms of Service'. The duty of the chairman at this stage of the investigation is of course purely to determine whether there is a *prima facie* case to go before the Service Committee, and the question which the Committee then has to decide is whether or not there has been a breach of the Terms of Service. It was obvious therefore that the Chairman had determined in his own mind the question upon which he was later to adjudicate. A letter was therefore addressed to him pointing this out and making it clear that in any future proceedings it might be necessary to make reference to the opinion he had so unfortunately expressed. It was imagined that the Chairman would realise his error and vacate the Chair for the hearing of this particular case. In the event, however, a very different view was taken by the Family Practitioner Committee, who decided that the protection society's letter to the Chairman was an 'unwarranted intrusion in the affairs of their Service Committee'. The letter informing the protection society of this remarkable view went on to state that a copy was being forwarded to the Minister and that it might be construed as an attempt to influence the result of the hearing, although indeed the Service Committee had meanwhile determined that the member was not in breach of his terms of service. In reply an assurance was given that, far from attempting to influence the finding of the Service Committee, the action of the protection society had been in the interests of the Chairman, for had the matter been ignored and the case later come to appeal, his action must inevitably have been severely criticised. Therefore, further observations were sought but no reply was received. After a suitable delay a letter was addressed to the Minister, pointing out that it would seem that the Family Practitioner Committee still failed to see anything in the least improper in the chairman of the Service Committee stating his opinion of a case which was later to come before the Committee for decision, and asking what action the Minister had taken regarding the copy of the letter which had been sent to him. In reply it was stated that while the Minister was not satisfied that the Chairman's letter should be interpreted as prejudging the issue—no other possible interpretation was put forward—he, the Minister, had suggested to

Table 10.1 Family Practitioner Committee Services Service committee cases: England

		1975	*1976*	*1977*
General medical services				
Disciplinary action–cases investigated	Total	545	587	596
No breach found		453	506	511
Breach found		92	81	85
Decisions to withhold remuneration	Total	23	21	25
Amounts–under £100		9	8	14
£100 to £249		10	10	3
£250 and over		4	3	8
Representations made against withholdings		2(1)	—	6(4)
No. of reductions following representations		—	—	2
Appeals against decisions of Family Practitioner Committees	Total	85(40)	65(30)	110(33)
Appeals by complainant		65(21)	52(20)	93(23)
Appeals by practitioner		20(19)	13(10)	17(10)
Appeals allowed to complainant		3(2)	6(6)	7(6)
Appeals allowed to practitioner		4(4)	4(3)	8(6)

the Committee that it was desirable that when a Chairman of a Service Committee sees correspondence of this nature he should not go beyond giving the opinion required by the Rules.

The figures shown in Table 10.1 need little comment. The selection of cases is clearly inadequate.The small proportion of cases in which doctors were fined illustrates how few of the offences were other than technical, and considering that there are over 26 000 general practitioners in England and Wales, it is apparent that the care they provide is of a very high standard.

What figures cannot show is the effect of this system upon the doctor. Only those who have been privileged to assist their colleagues in these matters can fully appreciate the toll taken by an entirely groundless complaint, on the health and strength of a conscientious, hard-worked practitioner. Throughout many months he is subjected to worry and anxiety which cannot but affect the quality of his work. He cannot, perhaps, look for any consideration from the Secretary of State who will, not infrequently, take six months or more to announce the result of an appeal, but it should be very apparent that a worried doctor is a less than fully efficient doctor, and it follows that to allow one malcontent to influence adversely a doctor's care of all his patients cannot in the long run be in the interests of the National Health Service.

11 The General Medical Council

The General Medical Council has duties respecting registration, education and professional discipline. Education does not concern us here; admission to the Register has been dealt with in the first chapter, and this chapter will be concerned only with remaining on it once one has achieved that goal. The Medical Register, which deals solely with details of the doctors' registration, should not be confused with that unofficial but more informative publication, the Medical Directory. When wishing to confirm that an individual is a registered medical practitioner one consults the former, when wishing to know what posts a doctor may have held in the past the information will be found in the latter.

Disciplinary Jurisdiction

The manner in which the GMC carries out its disciplinary jurisdiction is laid down in the Medical Act 1978 which follows to a considerable extent the recommendations of the Merrison Commission. Convictions in the criminal courts and complaints of alleged serious professional misconduct, if not disregarded as trivial or dismissed with a warning letter, come before the Preliminary Proceedings Committee. This Committee has the duty of deciding whether a case need be considered by either the Professional Conduct Committee or the Health Committee, which is the same thing as saying that erasure from the Register, suspension of registration, or making registration subject to conditions, might be considered to be the appropriate penalty, or remedy. The Preliminary Proceedings Committee may simply issue a warning letter, it may refer to the Professional Conduct Committee, or the Health Committee, and it may order immediate interim suspension, or immediate conditional registration, laying down under what conditions registration may be continued. Before imposing an interim suspension or interim conditional registration order, the Committee must give the doctor the opportunity of being heard as to whether or not such order should be imposed. An appeal against such an interim order lies to the High Court.

The Professional Conduct Committee, having satisfied itself regarding a conviction, or having judged that a doctor is guilty of serious professional misconduct, may order erasure, suspension of registration for a period not exceeding twelve months, or that the doctor's registration be made subject to certain conditions for a period of up to three years. Not every conviction or finding of serious professional misconduct need lead to one of these penalties, for the Committee may consider that the doctor's appearance before them has been punishment enough, and frequently will take the intermediate course of postponing judgment for a year or more whilst requiring the doctor then to produce evidence of his conduct in the meantime. Periods of suspension and conditional registration may be extended, and suspension may be followed by a period of conditional registration. A failure to comply with conditions imposed can lead to erasure or suspension.

The Health Committee is a new creation under the 1978 Medical Act. Its function is to determine whether a doctor's fitness to practise is seriously impaired by his physical or mental condition. It has no power of erasure but may suspend registration for successive periods of up to twelve months and impose conditions on future registration for a period not exceeding three years, extendable annually. At the time of writing, the Health Committee, after many years of consideration of the sick doctor problem, is just about to commence operations. The manner in which it will set about its task is worth noting in some detail.

The procedure is set in motion by the receipt by the GMC in writing of information which questions whether a doctor's fitness to practise is seriously impaired by reason of his physical or mental condition. Unless the information comes from a person acting in a public capacity, or from a hospital Medical Staff Committee, it must be in the form of a statutory declaration giving the name and address of the informant.

This information is first considered by the President, and unless thought to be trivial, the doctor is notified of the allegations, asked to agree to examination and report by two doctors appointed by the President, and invited to submit his own observations or evidence including reports by other doctors who have examined him.

The President then considers the reports and has copies sent to the practitioner. Should it be that there is a unanimous opinion that the doctor is not fit to practise, or to practise only on a limited basis, or should there be a difference of opinion and it appears to the President that the doctor is unfit, then the doctor is asked whether he will accept the recommendations of the examiners, including any limitations on practise which are recommended.

Where the doctor accepts the recommendations, further action is postponed, but otherwise the President confers with two other members of the Council appointed for the purpose, and a decision is taken on whether a case should be referred to the Health Committee.

The Health Committee sits in private with one or more medical assessors. The doctor is entitled to be present, and may be represented by a relative, his defence society or lawyer, and may bring his own medical adviser. Following the hearing the Committee determines whether the doctor's fitness to practise is seriously impaired by reason of his physical or mental condition, and if so whether, for a period of up to three years, the doctor's registration should be subject to such conditions as the Committee may impose. Alternatively the Committee may suspend the doctor for up to twelve months. The period of suspension and conditional registration may in appropriate cases be extended.

Apart from cases sent originally, or via the Preliminary Proceedings Committee to the Health Committee, the Professional Conduct Committee may also refer cases where that Committee considers that the doctor's state of health is a relevant issue and that treatment rather than punishment would be appropriate. Should the Health Committee find that the doctor's fitness to practise is not seriously impaired by his state of health, the Professional Conduct Committee is notified to this effect.

Both the Professional Conduct Committee and the Health Committee may, where erasure or suspension has been imposed, and where thought necessary for the protection of the public or in the doctor's own interests, order immediate suspension. Such orders are subject to appeal to the High Court—in Scotland to the Court of Session. Appeals otherwise—that is against erasure, suspension other than immediate suspension, or conditional registration—lie to the Judicial Committee of the Privy Council, and the doctor has 28 days within which to exercise his right of appeal. The Act specifies that no appeal lies against a decision of the Health Committee except on a question of law.

So much for the provisions of the Act. The doctor who finds himself in difficulty with the GMC should immediately get in touch with his protection society, who will deal with the correspondence and arrange his representation should he be required to attend before the Professional Conduct Committee or Health Committee.

Where the doctor has been convicted in a criminal court, he is not entitled to argue before the GMC that he was innocent of the charge. Following formal proof of the conviction and hearing any plea in mitigation of sentence, the Committee determines what action to take. It is because of this provision that doctors should be very careful indeed before pleading guilty to minor criminal charges with a view to getting a matter over cheaply and without publicity.

Where a case is one of conduct not conviction, then it is of course open to the defence to argue that the doctor did not act as alleged, that if he did so act then such acts do not amount to serious professional misconduct, and if that they are considered so to do, nevertheless erasure is not merited.

Following erasure, application for restoration to the Register may be made after not less than 10 months, though it is seldom advisable for the doctor to apply until a longer period has elapsed. Where the sentence is postponed the doctor will be instructed to appear before the Committee at a later date, having previously given the names of doctors and other persons of standing to whom the Committee can apply for information regarding the doctor's conduct in the interim. Where the Committee is not satisfied with the evidence regarding the doctor's conduct, e.g. where there has been a further conviction, or where the references are unsatisfactory, further postponement may be ordered.

The Professional Conduct Committee does not give reasons for its decisions. This fact, coupled with the repeatedly stated reluctance of the Judicial Committee of the Privy Council to upturn any decision of the GMC, renders the right of appeal of minimal value. A very unsatisfactory feature of the Act is the failure to give a right of appeal to the doctor adjudged guilty of serious professional misconduct, but neither erased nor suspended, nor subjected to conditional registration.

Types of Serious Professional Misconduct

There has come into being since the inception of the NHS a type of patient who considers that the doctor is there to comply with his every demand, and who is prone to threaten to report the doctor should the desired prescription or certificate not be forthcoming. The doctor need not worry about such threats from the lunatic fringe, nor is the GMC concerned with alleged minor infringements of the ethical code or of the NHS regulations. Even should a doctor be found to have been negligent in a civil action, this is most unlikely to bring him before the Professional Conduct Committee; for in the first place it is only criminal and not civil courts which as a routine report to the GMC, and secondly, while the GMC would certainly be concerned with a doctor's serious neglect of responsibilities towards his patients, if following neglect a claim in negligence was lodged, it would almost inevitably be settled out of Court. The fact that a case has gone into Court implies that there was a reasonable defence, so that the degree of negligence is very unlikely to be such as would concern the GMC.

Neglect of Patients

The GMC is not concerned with errors in diagnosis or treatment. It is rather the manner in which a practice is run or a hospital appointment carried out, whereby patients may be put at risk, that leads doctors to appear before the Professional Conduct Committee. Repeated failure to visit, improper delegation of medical duties, and unavailability when on duty, are examples of the types of neglect which could lead to a finding of serious professional misconduct.

Alcohol

The most common offences which the GMC have to consider are those arising from the abuse of alcohol. Where a doctor has been convicted it is no defence but merely a mitigating factor to point out that he was not on professional duty at the time the offence occurred, for convictions as opposed to matters of conduct do not need to be 'in a professional respect'. As a rule, a first conviction which does not involve any harm to a patient is dealt with by a warning letter, but should a second conviction follow the doctor may find himself before the Professional Conduct Committee, where both convictions will be considered. The line taken by the Professional Conduct Committee is usually that such convictions indicate habits which constitute a potential danger to patients, and the doctor will likely be put on 'probation'. Subsequent convictions or failure to provide the necessary testimonials regarding conduct, may well result in erasure or suspension. It is anticipated that a substantial proportion of these cases will in future come before the Health Committee.

Drugs

Abuse of drugs leads a number of doctors to come before the Professional Conduct Committee. Such cases are more varied than those involving alcohol, and all that can be said is that the doctor who has become addicted and who can show evidence of having made a determined effort to overcome his addiction can, whatever statutory offences his addiction has led him to, anticipate that he will be regarded as requiring help rather than punishment. Such will not however apply to one who has misused his position as a doctor to promote his own financial advantage by prescribing drugs of addiction without medical reason. Somewhere in between come those doctors who have allowed themselves to become soft touches for addicts, and any doctor who finds himself becoming involved with such people would do well to pay immediate heed to the warnings he is likely to receive from the Home Office Inspector.

Misleading Certificates

Reference has been made in the chapter on Criminal Law to the troubles which can follow the issue of a misleading or untrue certificate. The GMC tends to take a serious view of any laxity in this respect, and a doctor who has been convicted of such an offence may very possibly find himself placed on 'probation' by the Professional Conduct Committee. Repeated offences could doubtless lead to erasure.

Canvassing and Advertising

Canvassing for patients or employing persons to canvass for one or even acquiescing in such an activity may lead to erasure. In this respect it is of particular importance to observe carefully the regulations regarding the transfer of patients on a doctor's National Health Service list following his death or retirement. Advertising, which has been discussed in the chapter on Professional Ethics, may also bring a doctor before the Professional Conduct Committee.

The recent proliferation of clinics providing specialised services has led the GMC to issue advice on a doctor's relationship with them. Where the organisation advertises directly to the public, then the doctor who owns or holds shares should not work for the organisation in a clinical capacity, permit his professional qualifications to appear on advertising material, or be otherwise involved in advertising.

Doctors who work for such organisations must be remunerated on a sessional and not on a per capita basis. Where the organisation running the clinic or nursing home advertises only to the medical profession, the doctor who owns or holds shares in it should ensure that the advertisements do not infringe the general principles regarding advertising, and in particular do not make invidious comparisons with other organisations.

Miscellaneous Offences

Incorrect claims under the NHS regulations, improperly demanding money from NHS patients, prescribing drugs in which the doctor has a financial interest, commercialisation of a secret remedy, dichotomy, forgery, indecent behaviour, breach of professional secrecy, covering medical practice by an unregistered person, and depreciation of professional colleagues, are examples of other less common matters which concern the GMC. As such offences can vary from inadvertence to deliberate crime, so will the doctor receive anything from warning to erasure.

Sexual Misconduct with Patients

The classical example of serious professional misconduct is of course adultery with a patient, and perhaps the doctor's duty in respect of the trust placed in him was best summed up by the Judicial Committee of the Privy Council as follows:

> 'A doctor gains entry to the home in the trust that he will take care of the physical and mental health of the family. He must not abuse his professional position so as by act or word to impair in the least the confidence and security which should subsist between husband and wife. His association with the wife becomes improper when by look, touch, or gesture he shows undue affection for her, when he seeks opportunities of meeting her alone, or does anything else to show that he thinks more of her than he should. Even if she sets her cap at him, he must in no way respond or encourage her. If she seeks opportunities of meeting him which are not necessary for professional reasons, he must be on his guard. He must shun any association with her altogether rather than let it become improper. He must be above suspicion.

It was suggested that a doctor who was a family doctor might be in a different position when he became a family friend. His conduct on social occasions was to be regarded differently from his conduct on professional occasions. There must, it was said, be cogent evidence to show that he abused his professional position. It was not enough to show that he abused his social friendship. This looks very like a suggestion that he might do in the drawing room that which he might not do in the surgery. No such distinction can be permitted. A medical man who gains entry into the family confidence by virtue of his professional position must maintain the same high standard when he becomes the family friend.'

The offences mentioned above are of course but a sample and in no way an exhaustive list; indeed it would not be possible to draw up such a list, for times and conditions change. Who would think of including the offence of 'keeping and exhibiting an anatomical museum containing waxworks of a disgusting nature'? For this unique offence the name of a doctor was many years ago erased.

Composition and Duty of the GMC

The GMC is composed of 93 members, consisting of elected members, appointed members, and nominated members. The elected members, i.e. those elected by the profession, exceed the number of appointed and nominated members. Appointed members are chosen by universities and other bodies empowered to grant a registrable qualification. They and the elected members must be registered, fully, provisionally or with limited registration. Nominated members are nominated by Her Majesty on the advice of Her Privy Council, at least one each being nominated for England, for Wales, for Scotland, and for Northern Ireland. A majority of nominated members must be non-medical.

Branch Councils exist for England, Wales, Scotland and Northern Ireland, and consist of those members of the Council elected by, appointed for, or nominated for the relevant area.

The Preliminary Proceedings Committee consists of eleven members, the Professional Conduct Committee of twenty, of whom five make a quorum, and not more than ten hear any case. The Act requires that no member who sits as a member of the Preliminary Proceedings Committee on any case shall sit as a member of the

Professional Conduct Committee, or of the Health Committee on any subsequent proceedings on that case. The Health Committee consists of twelve members, of whom five constitute a quorum.

The predominance of medical members of the Council must, however, not leave one to suppose that it is in any sense an organisation for protecting the interests of doctors, or has the slightest bias in their favour. The Medical Act 1858 which brought the Council into being had as its prime object the protection of the public, and when considering whether a doctor's name should be erased from the Register, it is the interest of the public and not the interest of the doctor, nor the interest of the profession, which is uppermost in the Committee's mind.

Finally, the judicial definition of 'infamous conduct in a professional respect' persisted until the Medical Act 1969, and the modern phrase 'serious professional misconduct' differs from it in no significant respect. It was enunciated in 1894 by Lord Justice Lopes in the following words:

> 'If a medical man in the pursuit of his profession has done something with regard to it which will be reasonably regarded as disgraceful or dishonourable by his professional brethren of good repute and competency, then it is open to the General Medical Council, if that be shown, to say that he has been guilty of infamous conduct in a professional respect.'

Lord Esher gave as his opinion: 'The question is not merely whether what the medical man has done would be an infamous thing for anyone else but a medical man to do. He might do an infamous thing which would be infamous in anyone else, but if it is not done in a professional respect it does not come within the Section.' These observations have great authority, but of recent years there has perhaps been a tendency to put a very wide definition on what can be considered serious professional misconduct, so much so, that even leaving aside all other considerations there is much to be said for doctors refraining from serious misconduct of any nature whatsoever.

Appendix A **Declarations of The World Medical Association**

Declaration of Helsinki

Recommendations guiding medical doctors in biomedical research involving human subjects, adopted by the 18th World Medical Assembly, Helsinki, Finland, 1964 and as revised by the 29th World Medical Assembly, Tokyo, Japan, 1975.

Introduction

It is the mission of the medical doctor to safeguard the health of the people. His or her knowledge and conscience are dedicated to the fulfilment of this mission.

The Declaration of Geneva of the World Medical Association binds the doctor with the world. 'The health of my patient will be my first consideration', and the International Code of Medical Ethics declares that, 'Any act or advice which could weaken physical or mental resistance of a human being may be used only in his interest'.

The purpose of biomedical research involving human subjects must be to improve diagnostic, therapeutic and prophylactic procedures and the understanding of the aetiology and pathogenesis of disease.

In current medical practice most diagnostic, therapeutic or prophylactic procedures involve hazards. This applies *a fortiori* to biomedical research.

Medical progress is based on research which ultimately must rest in part on experimentation involving human subjects.

In the field of biomedical research a fundamental distinction must be recognised between medical research in which the aim is essentially diagnostic or therapeutic for a patient, and medical research, the essential object of which is purely scientific and without direct diagnostic or therapeutic value to the person subjected to the research.

Special caution must be exercised in the conduct of research which may affect the environment, and the welfare of animals used for research must be respected.

Because it is essential that the results of laboratory experiments be applied to human beings to further scientific knowledge and to help suffering humanity, the World Medical Association has prepared the following recommendations as a guide to every doctor in biomedical research involving human subjects. They should be kept under review in the future. It must be stressed that the standards as drafted are only a guide to physicians all over the world. Doctors are not relieved from criminal, civil and ethical responsibilities under the laws of their own countries.

I Basic principles

1 Biomedical research involving human subjects must conform to generally accepted scientific principles and should be based on adequately performed laboratory and animal experimentation and on a thorough knowledge of the scientific literature.

2 The design and performance of each experimental procedure involving human subjects should be clearly formulated in an experimental protocol which should be transmitted to a specially appointed independent committee for consideration, comment and guidance.

3 Biomedical research involving human subjects should be conducted only by scientifically qualified persons and under the supervision of a clinically competent medical person. The responsibility for the human subject must always rest with a medically qualified person and never rest on the subject of the research, even though the subject has given his or her consent.

4 Biomedical research involving human subjects cannot legitimately be carried out unless the importance of the objective is in proportion to the inherent risk to the subject.

5 Every biomedical research project involving human subjects should be preceded by careful assessment of predictable risks in comparison with forseeable benefits to the subject or to others. Concern for the interests of the subject must always prevail over the interests of science and society.

6 The right of the research subject to safeguard his or her integrity must always be respected. Every precaution should be taken to respect the privacy of the subject and to minimise the impact of

the study on the subject's physical and mental integrity and on the personality of the subject.

7 Doctors should abstain from engaging in research projects involving human subjects unless they are satisfied that the hazards involved are believed to be predictable. Doctors should cease any investigation if the hazards are found to outweigh the potential benefits.

8 In publication of the results of his or her research, the doctor is obliged to preserve the accuracy of the results. Reports of experimentation not in accordance with the principles laid down in this Declaration should not be accepted for publication.

9 In any research on human beings, each potential subject must be adequately informed of the aims, methods, anticipated benefits and potential hazards of the study and the discomfort it may entail. He or she should be informed that he or she is at liberty to abstain from participation in the study and that he or she is free to withdraw his or her consent to participation at any time. The doctor should then obtain the subject's freely-given informed consent, preferably in writing.

10 When obtaining informed consent for the research project the doctor should be particularly cautious if the subject is in a dependent relationship to him or her or may consent under duress. In that case the informed consent should be obtained by a doctor who is not engaged in the investigation and who is completely independent of this official relationship.

11 In case of legal incompetence, informed consent should be obtained from the legal guardian in accordance with national legislation. Where physical or mental incapacity make it impossible to obtain informed consent, or when the subject is a minor, permission from the responsible relative replaces that of the subject in accordance with national legislation.

12 The research protocol should always contain a statement of the ethical considerations involved and should indicate that the principles enunciated in the present Declaration are complied with.

II Medical Research Combined with Professional Care (Clinical Research)

1 In the treatment of the sick person, the doctor must be free to use a new diagnostic and therapeutic measure, if in his or her judgment it offers hope of saving life, re-establishing health or alleviating suffering.

2 The potential benefits, hazards and discomfort of a new method should be weighed against the advantages of the best current diagnostic and therapeutic methods.
3 In any medical study, every patient—including those of a control group, if any—should be assured of the best proven diagnostic and therapeutic method.
4 The refusal of the patient to participate in a study must never interfere with the doctor–patient relationship.
5 If the doctor considers it essential not to obtain informed consent, the specific reasons for this proposal should be stated in the experimental protocol for transmission to the independent committee (I, 2).
6 The doctor can combine medical research with professional care, the objective being the acquisition of new medical knowledge, only to the extent that medical research is justified by its potential diagnostic or therapeutic value for the patient.

III Non-Therapeutic Biomedical Research Involving Human Subjects (Non-Clinical Biomedical Research)

1 In the purely scientific application of medical research carried out on a human being, it is the duty of the doctor to remain the protector of the life and health of that person on whom biomedical research is being carried out.
2 The subjects should be volunteers—either healthy persons or patients for whom the experimental design is not related to the patient's illness.
3 The investigator or the investigating team should discontinue the research if in his/her or their judgment it may, if continued, be harmful to the individual.
4 In research on man, the interest of science and society should never take precedence over considerations related to the well being of the subject.

Declaration of Sydney

Statement on death adopted by the 22nd World Medical Assembly, Sydney, Australia, August 1968.

1 The determination of the time of death is in most countries the legal responsibility of the physician and should remain so. Usually

he will be able without special assistance to decide that a person is dead, employing the classical criteria known to all physicians.

2 Two modern practices in medicine, however, have made it necessary to study the question of the time of death further: (a) the ability to maintain by artificial means the circulation of oxygenated blood through tissues of the body which may have been irreversibly injured and (b) the use of cadaver organs such as heart or kidneys for transplantation.

3 A complication is that death is a gradual process at the cellular level with tissues varying in their ability to withstand deprivation of oxygen. But clinical interest lies not in the state of preservation of isolated cells but in the fate of a person. Here the point of death *of the different cells and organs* is not so important as the certainty that the process has become irreversible by whatever techniques of resuscitation may be employed.

4 This determination will be based on clinical judgment supplemented *if necessary* by a number of diagnostic aids of which the electroencephalograph is currently the most helpful. However, no single technological criterion is entirely satisfactory in the present state of medicine nor can any one technological procedure be substituted for the overall judgment of the physician. *If transplantation of an organ is involved, the decision that death exists should be made by two or more physicians and the physicians determining the moment of death should in no way be immediately concerned with performance of transplantation.*

5 Determination of the point of death of the person makes it ethically permissible to cease attempts at resuscitation and in countries where the law permits, to remove organs from the cadaver provided that prevailing requirements of consent have been fulfilled.

Declaration of Oslo

Statement on therapeutic abortion adopted by the 24th World Medical Assemly, Oslo, Norway, 1970.

1 The first moral principle imposed upon the doctor is respect for human life as expressed in a clause of the Declaration of Geneva: 'I will maintain the utmost respect for human life from the time of conception'.

2 Circumstances which bring the vital interest of a mother into conflict with the vital interests of her unborn child create a dilemma and raise the question whether or not the pregnancy should be deliberately terminated.
3 Diversity of response to this situation results from the diversity of attitudes towards the life of the unborn child. This is a matter of individual conviction and conscience which must be respected.
4 It is not the role of the medical profession to determine the attitudes and rules of any particular state or community in this matter, but it is our duty to attempt both to ensure the protection of our patients and to safeguard the rights of the doctor within society.
5 Therefore, where the law allows therapeutic abortion to be performed, or legislation to that effect is contemplated, and this is not against the policy of the national medical association, and where the legislature desires or will accept the guidance of the medical profession, the following principles are approved:
   (a) Abortion should be performed only as a therapeutic measure.
   (b) A decision to terminate pregnancy normally should be approved in writing by at least two doctors chosen for their professional competence.
   (c) The procedure should be performed by a doctor competent to do so in premises approved by the appropriate authority.
6 If a doctor considers that his convictions do not allow him to advise or perform an abortion, he may withdraw while ensuring the continuity of (medical) care by a qualified colleague.
7 This statement, while it is endorsed by the General Assembly of the World Medical Association, is not to be regarded as binding on any individual member association unless it is adopted by that member association.

Declaration of Tokyo

Guidelines for medical doctors concerning torture and other cruel, inhuman or degrading treatment or punishment in relation to detention and imprisonment, as adopted by the 29th World Medical Assembly, Tokyo, Japan, October 1975.

It is the privilege of the medical doctor to practise medicine in the service of humanity, to preserve and restore bodily and mental health without distinction as to persons, to comfort, and to ease the suffering of his or her patients. The utmost respect for human life is to be maintained even under threat, and no use made of any medical knowledge contrary to the laws of humanity.

For the purpose of this Declaration torture is defined as the deliberate, systematic or wanton infliction of physical or mental suffering by one or more persons acting alone or on the orders of any authority, to force another to yield information, to make a confession, or for any other reason.

Declaration

1 The doctor shall not countenance, condone or participate in the practice of torture or other forms of cruel, inhuman or degrading procedures, whatever the offence of which the victim of such procedures is suspected, accused or guilty, and whatever the victim's beliefs or motives, and in all situations, including armed conflict and civil strife.
2 The doctor shall not provide any premises, instruments, substances or knowledge to facilitate the practice of torture or other forms of cruel, inhuman or degrading treatment or to diminish the ability of the victim to resist such treatment.
3 The doctor shall not be present during any procedure during which torture or other forms of cruel, inhuman or degrading treatment is used or threatened.
4 A doctor must have complete clinical independence in deciding upon the care of a person for whom he or she is medically responsible. The doctor's fundamental role is to alleviate the distress of his or her fellow men, and no motive whether personal, collective or political shall prevail against this higher purpose.
5 Where a prisoner refuses nourishment and is considered by the doctor as capable of forming an unimpaired and rational judgment concerning the consequences of such a voluntary refusal of nourishment, he or she shall not be fed artificially. The decision as to the capacity of the prisoner to form such a judgment should be confirmed by at least one other independent doctor. The consequences of the refusal of nourishment shall be explained by the doctor to the prisoner.
6 The World Medical Association will support, and should encourage the international community, the national medical associations and fellow doctors, to support the doctor and his or her family in the face of threats or reprisals resulting from a refusal to

condone the use of torture or other forms of cruel, inhuman or degrading treatment.

Declaration of Lisbon

On the rights of the patient adopted by the 34th World Medical Assembly, Lisbon, Portugal, September/October 1981.

Recognising that there may be practical, ethical or legal difficulties, a physician should always act according to his/her conscience and always in the best interest of the patient. The following Declaration represents some of the principal rights which the medical profession seeks to provide to patients.

Whenever legislation or government action denies these rights of the patient, physicians should seek by appropriate means to assure or to restore them.

a The patient has the right to choose his physician freely.
b The patient has the right to be cared for by a physician who is free to make clinical and ethical judgments without any outside interference.
c The patient has the right to accept or to refuse treatment after receiving adequate information.
d The patient has the right to expect that his physician will respect the confidential nature of all his medical and personal details.
e The patient has the right to die in dignity.
f The patient has the right to receive or to decline spiritual and moral comfort including the help of a minister of an appropriate religion.

Appendix B **Guidelines to aid Ethical Committees considering Research involving Children**

(published by The British Paediatric Association in 1980)

These guidelines presume that four premises are accepted.

That research involving children is important for the benefit of all children and should be supported and encouraged and conducted in an ethical manner.

That research should never be done on children if the same investiation could be done on adults.

That research which involves a child and is of no benefit to that child (non-therapeutic research) is not necessarily either unethical or illegal.

That the degree of benefit resulting from a research should be assessed in relation to the risk of disturbance, discomfort, or pain—the risk : benefit ratio.

Defining 'Risk'

Risk, in this context, means the risk of causing physical disturbance, discomfort or pain, or psychological disturbance to the child or his parents, rather than the risk of serious harm, which no Ethical Committee would countenance in any case.

Negligible risk—Risk less than that run in everyday life.

Minimal risk—Risk questionably greater than negligible risk.

More than minimal risk.

Defining 'Benefit'

Non-therapeutic Research

a The procedure is of no benefit to the subject but may benefit the health and welfare of other children or adults. A special case, but an important one, is if the subject suffers from a disorder and the research aims to benefit others suffering from a similar disorder.

b The procedure is of no benefit to the subject but may add to basic biological knowledge—for example, normal values of aging.

Therapeutic Research
The procedure is of potential benefit to the subject.

Applying the Risk: Benefit Principle in Non-therapeutic Research

Procedures requiring ethical judgments are usually those which are without benefit to the subject—non-therapeutic research. Most such procedures will fall into one of the following three categories.

1 The procedure is either (a) part of the ordinary care of the infant or child (weighing, measuring, feeding), or (b) involves the non-invasive collection of samples—for example, urine, faeces, saliva, hair or nail clippings, or, at birth, cord blood or placental tissue. Risk is here likely to be negligible—for example, test weighing a breast-fed baby as part of a study aimed to promote breast feeding.

2 The procedure involves invasive collection of samples—for example, blood, cerebrospinal fluid, or biopsy tissue—taken from a child who is undergoing treatment. The sample used for research may be (a) an additional amount to that required on clinical grounds; or (b) not an ordinary part of the child's treatment—for example, collection of biopsy material during a surgical operation. Risk in (a) might be either negligible or minimal; (b) might be negligible, minimal, or more than minimal.

Examples
In cystic fibrosis, a research might be considered reasonable which involved an affected child having a sweat test that needed twice as much sweat as required for purely diagnostic purposes. The added discomfort to the child might be assessed as negligible. If in addition a venepuncture was required, this might be judged to put the risk of discomfort and pain into the minimal risk category. But the potential benefit to other child sufferers from this common and serious disease might be deemed such as to make the risk: benefit ratio acceptable.

During the course of an operation for hernia, a fragment of skin from the incision might be required for a research involving tissue culture. The risk could be judged negligible, so that even if the research was not expected to have any direct clinical benefit but only to add to basic biological knowledge, it might be acceptable.

During the course of an abdominal operation, a renal biopsy might be taken for research purposes. The risk here would be judged more than minimal and the benefit would have to be very large to justify it. But suppose the research aimed to resolve the problem of rejection of transplanted kidneys, with resulting lifesaving consequences both for children and adults with renal failure; this might be considered a benefit of sufficient magnitude to justify the risk.

3 The procedure is quite apart from the necessary care or treatment of the child. For example, blood sampling; passage of oesophageal tube for pressure recording; application of face mask for respiration studies; placement of infant in plethysmograph chamber for thermal or respiratory studies; needle biopsy of skin or fat; or X-ray or isotope studies (see below). The risk might be negligible, minimal, or more than minimal. The benefit, as defined above in relation to non-therapeutic research, may fall within either the definition (a) or (b). If it comes under definition (a), the risk should, to be acceptable, probably be either negligible or minimal. If the benefit comes under definition (b), the risk should be negligible.

Examples
In thalassaemia, a common and lethal disease, progress might depend on taking blood specimens from both affected and unaffected children. The benefit could be assessed as great, so justifying the risk of causing more than minimal discomfort or pain to the children.

Many diabetic children will develop blindness or other severe eye complications in adult life. A research aimed at eventually learning how to prevent this might require several glucose tolerance tests to be done on a diabetic child, not for his own benefit but for the benefit of other diabetic children. The risk of discomfort or pain to that child would be assessed as more than minimal, but might nevertheless be justified by the potential benefit.

The physiology of the initiation of breathing by the baby at birth is poorly understood, and is of clinical importance because some babies fail to breathe. A study of normal newborn babies' first breath, using a face mask, may be judged to cause minimal risk with a justifiable risk:benefit ratio.

Applying the Risk:Benefit Principle in Therapeutic Research

Therapeutic research offers potential benefit to the subject. It includes not only trials of new drugs or procedures but also trials of therapies which, though perhaps widely applied, are yet of unproved value. The risk:benefit principle may still be applicable, the potential benefit as well as the risk relating to the individual subject.

In general, ethical principles in therapeutic research involving children do not usually differ from those applying to adults, except that the age of the subject will often mean that parental understanding and agreement will be required.

In the common type of experiment where two therapies are compared in a controlled trial, two ethical questions are likely to arise.

1 Is the research necessary? For instance, conventional treatment of a febrile convulsion in a child includes drastic cooling. A research project might question this form of management and entail a controlled trial. An Ethical Committee might consider it probable that data already existed enabling the question to be answered. The Committee might therefore require the researcher first to provide evidence that the world literature had been effectively searched.
2 Is the design of the trial such that a statistically significant result will emerge with the use of a minimal number of subjects and in a minimum period? Since one set of children will receive what may eventually turn out to be an inferior therapy, it is ethically imperative that this question be answered in the affirmative.

Examples

Current research in treating leukaemia in children often means comparing two different drug regimens. Since both sets of children receive therapies currently considered acceptable, ethical considerations are mainly confined to ensuring that the design of the trial is statistically sound.

A controlled trial of hyposensitising injections of allergens in asthmatic children differs from the foregoing example in that some children (the controls) receive injections of inactive material. This might at first sight seem ethically questionable. However, the following consideration may lead to such a trial being judged acceptable. Until the result of the trial is known the children in either the treatment or the control group have a chance of gaining an advantage. The active therapy may prove superior and those in the treatment group gain an advantage. If, however, there are unpleasant or harmful side effects from the active therapy, the control group will have gained some advantage by not being exposed to those side effects.

X-rays and Isotopes

An authoritative pronouncement on the ethical propriety of irradiating children—that is, the use of X-rays or isotopes—for research purposes has recently been given by the International Commission on Radiological Protection. It states that 'the irradiation, for the purposes of such studies (that is, of no direct benefit to the subject) of children and other persons regarded as being incapable of giving their true consent should only be undertaken if the expected radiation is low (for example, of the order of one-10th of the dose-equivalent limits applicable to individual members of the public) and if valid approval has been given by those legally responsible for such persons'.

This means, in common parlance, that exposure to X-rays could be justifiable where the dosage was comparable to the normal variation in natural irradiation received by, say, individuals living in two different parts of the British Isles. In fact, using modern equipment, a single radiograph might fall well within such dosage limits, and thus, be classifiable as a negligible risk.

Parental Permission and Cooperation. Agreement by the Child

Parental (or guardian's) permission should normally be obtained—with rare exceptions such as the comparison of two treatments for some emergency condition—after explaining as fully as possible the nature of the procedure. Whether or not this should be a signed, witnessed declaration remains debatable. It is an advantage if the parents can be present during the procedure. Although the law in Britain does not recognise an age of consent, children much younger than 16 often have enough understanding to collaborate altruistically in a project.

New Drugs: New Immunisation Procedures

In general these should be first tested on animals, then on adult volunteers, then on older children able to take part voluntarily in the research, and only then on younger children.

Index to Cases

Table of Statutes

General Index